# Sweet Not Stupid

## HOW TO FIND YOUR VOICE THROUGH THE POWER OF POETRY

Tamara Faith

Paperback ISBN: 978-1-63616-030-6
Ebook ISBN: 978-1-63616-039-9

Published by Opportune Independent Publishing Company

For permission requests, write to the publisher, addressed "Attention: Permissions Coordinator" to the address below.

Email: Info@opportunepublishing.com

Address: 113 N. Live Oak Street
Houston, TX 77003

# CONTENTS

# DEDICATION

This book is dedicated to those who have not yet found the power in their voice. I want you to know that no matter where you find yourself, your voice matters and you have what it takes to express yourself. You don't have to be over the top, loud or abrasive in your delivery. Your world will receive you just as you are. I see you, and you are not alone. And always remember, "meek is not weak, and Sweet is just as strong."

# ACKNOWLEDGMENTS

Often times, we don't take the time to look back at the experiences that have made us who we are. Each upset, each downfall, each setback, all were actually a set up for a greater outcome, and they contribute to the greatness that we step into each day. We need to take a step back and look at how each experience taught us to step up and utilize what was at our disposal to express ourselves in a strong light. Everything in life, from breakups to communication errors, to misunderstandings with the opposite sex, all contribute to building our characters.

All the failed relationships, all the friendships and family drama has pushed me in my own life to find my voice. It was difficult for a while. First, I had to recognize the power I possessed, then I had to exercise it, and take notice of others and allow them to exercise the same. Not only did I have to open my eyes for myself but also for others alongside me. I would not be before you today had it not been for God's grace. I can say that God's hand has been on my life, and he's been showing me how to find my voice. Seeing me through the difficulties of finding myself in an ever changing social climate.

God also gave me a group of friends to express myself and an unapologetic environment to show me what it meant to utilize my gift of the spoken word to get things off my chest. God already qualified me, and he showed me that I was enough. I have to acknowledge my mentors that guided me in the spoken word community. Samantha Liu, your support and leadership has helped me more than you know.

Ultimately, I have to give the biggest thank you to my loving and God-fearing parents and siblings who really encouraged me to step out of the box and write this book. They really do inspire me to be my best self and stretch past my limits. They really do have my back when I fall, and I really wouldn't be here without them. I also want to thank my writing coach Nikkie Pryce. She pushed me past my limits and believed in my efforts all the way. Thank you so much for everything. I pray that God blesses you beyond measure because you are more than deserving. This too is your season and I cannot wait for all that is to come!

# CHAPTER 1
# SILENCE

Silence itself can be deadly. It is the culprit of one's belief's being released. It can rob you of your ability to express yourself and, not long after, breed itself into regret. Regret of not being real, not taking advantage of the opportunity to share oneself. On the other hand, this very fear can make someone feel as though they have no safe place to release what's inside. It is important that we understand what happens amid the silence.

A mixture of negative effects along with outcomes that can prove to be empowering. Many of the negative outcomes or experiences include but are not limited to the following; pain, indecision, mystery, loss of identity, mental cloudiness and even a violent internal struggle to be seen or heard by our loved ones and peers. On the other hand, there is a stand that silence offers that we often don't give light to. That silence gives power that has already been shared and what has yet to be expressed. This, in turn, calls the environment and those in it to pay attention to the air of silence and prompting them to take each opportunity of expression seriously. Silence itself has its place and is often the byproduct of our experiences. In this section, such poems have been written to shed light on what happens in the midst of silence.

Such experiences shared exposes pain, heartache and the internal struggle while offering tactics on how to fight the hindering feelings that linger as a result of such neglect. As you read this section, allow such feelings to hold the meaning you need it to. Be one with what is and find refuge in what can be done to fight through the silent moments we feel daily we otherwise think we cannot overcome. The truth is, we can and we will. And we can do it well. All in due time.

# Lets Identify

How does one enter into the permanence of silence? That the declaration of such a sentiment really seems to be the only outlet that offers a ready solution. That such removal makes the introduction of the pursuit that we were looking for.

What is the driving force of silence? What influences someone to withdraw their voice and their ready opinion to their outside world when it mattered the most? Is it the fear of being judged? Or an unsafe environment where one may feel rushed? Or the possibility of being embarrassed, leaving one blushed? There is a concern that meets us deep within. Where can we find refuge? And why are we being dismissed? Is it the energy?

Meshing oil and water, we are not left mixed with an adversary. Thoughts that contradict our own and make us feel unworthy. A seed of suppression that can breed a seed of aggression. The craze that can breed violence. Furniture toppling over, dishes crashing against the table, voices would emerge if they were able, but the channel seems to be lost. We don't have access to this cable. That such a message isn't being taken seriously instead, it feels like a fable.

Let's identify.

What's the why? Why does someone enter into the cave of silence? Risk that the rubble of the ceiling might fall on what we truly believe in. Shutting up and shutting down, the confidence we hold dear is nowhere to be found. I am aware. That feeling of being so alone and scared. I wonder… how long can we live there? Do we even wish to thrive there? Are we fooling ourselves? Can this life be compared to the joy that we know can meet us there? I am aware. The isolation silence can bring. Harboring one's own thoughts and ideas. Not knowing if anyone truly cared to begin with. What we fail to realize is that the push back, the resistance is being shared. Internal and external an unlikely pair. I admonish you, be careful. Unlikely weeds can be found here. Let's identify.

It is hardly fair to be considered so different and fearing no one else cares. That no one gives attention to that which you mention. I am aware. This place too, I've been there. Silence makes one feel all alone. Taking notice of anxious moments instead of calm. I urge you it isn't the end. And that I, too, understand.

This storm will cease, and others will keep you warm.

# The Void

There seems to be a place I always go that no one has caught onto yet. Hiding in plane sight, it has occurred to me that no one is used to my new disguise. My mind. I am but a figure, just figuring out life. Just like you are. I have yet to take form and offer the world my well-thought opinion. My words hold such weight and bright enough to make envy of the sun. So much so that it even scares me. I guess no matter the strength of the warmth, they are still finding their way out of my lips. Until then, I hide. Like a school kid, I wait on the world to call on me. It hasn't happened yet, so I sit, and I learn. Gathering as much information as I can.

Studious, up front, quiet and out of the way. I took notes with my ears and wrote down what made sense with my actions. I replayed what worked with my eyes and did away with the rest. I learned all there needed to be at the time until there was nothing left. I became the master at a young age. A guru in my own right.

Yet, I found refuge in my favorite hiding place. And

part of me is happy that no one has caught onto me just yet. Part of me aches for understanding. One chance, one shot to give it all I've got, yet it hasn't happened yet. I've always wanted to do such great things, but there seems to be a void between where I am and where I want to be. How do I get out? I've seemed to live with this internal struggle for what feels like forever. Although I can't help it, I noticed this has not done me any good whatsoever.

I am in a routine because silence seems to be the right thing. Distance from others seems to be helping but is actually causing a sting in my heart, and I'm looking to finding a new start. It starts with a decision in my heart. A resolve. The strongest conviction one could have. And it starts today. Today I want to stop hiding. I don't want to take the notes on life I'll never use. I want to use my voice like I know I should. I'll pinpoint the void I've been operating from and fill it with something new. Encouragement, hope and a new point of view. I'll try this out for myself, and soon I'll come back to help you too.

# The Real You

You've always known me. I do my best to make myself known, but you shut me out. With hands shaped like the hours and minutes, time passes until we are no longer well-acquainted. We have become mere strangers. I have taken a seat at the table I've set for us two, so we could get to know each other better. But with each voice that enters, they have become personified, taking raw form and growing limbs. Strong and able-bodied, making it much easier to roam about until they've made themselves at home. They are your insecurities. Your mistakes were mistaken for wrong seasons for all the wrong reasons. Your experiences, your failed relationships, your resolve that looks nothing like us. You've embraced them, but I know you best! I know that your heart is in the right place and not tainted by the rest.

I've always known you. I did my best to make myself known, but you just shut me out. With each space filled, seat after seat, occupied by someone we don't know. They've barged in and made themselves at home. And it's crowded now. What used to feel like peace has now ceased. What used to rest in sanity has now created calamity. Sadness, Madness, Anger, depression, aggression and I never wanted that for you. I never wanted that for us.

What happened to us? We've always known each other, and we haven't spoken in a while. But that isn't your fault. It became overwhelming, and it stopped you in your tracks. Anxiety has a way of doing that. But I never gave up on you. I never gave up on us. I was patient and gave you the time you needed. You used to be so bold and speak your mind. Now you've become so mild and tired, sometimes even cold. I always wanted more for you. More space to clearly see your face. So I took it upon myself to let our overwhelming guests out. One by one, one step at a time. Slowly but surely, instead of building walls, I cast safety nets so when the walls came down, we'd always find each other after the rubble cleared.

It was time you came back to you. And I was always here to receive you. Come back to yourself. Because yourself knows you best.

# Gentleness

This touch seems to be the most familiar. Being able to handle those around us that need it the most. A soft touch, a helping hand, I never thought I'd be here again. Pouring out your heart, your head on my shoulder. I pour into your heart as I give you the strength to start over. Assisting you in hard times because that's what good friends do. And all the while it fulfills me and makes me happy. I've recognized I've had a more difficult time adapting.

The gentleness I give freely, I never have enough left over. In time I'm learning. I have to give the same gentleness I have for others to myself. It's easy to pick up being hard on yourself because you want everything in order. Proving you're a good kid and you remember what your parents taught you. And it's true. Some fall short and aren't always treated the same. But it's true that not everyone deserves the harsh blame. We all make mistakes and but remember, we are all granted grace. In those moments when the hardship is hard to face, stop what's going on and slower your pace.
Become self-aware of what you need at the moment.

Is it a hug or immediate self-care? And be proactive about it, don't deny yourself any longer. Gentleness with yourself is the first step in getting stronger. It's about time we put into practice the right self-care.

# The Fight Within

Can you hear me? The gnashing of my teeth and the bite back of my cheeks. I have something to say. Clenched fists and blood rushing past my eyelids in the form of tears and crystal blue water, my pain is pure. And I bruise easily. I'll take accountability. Some of my wounds are self-inflicted. My wrists have rings from holding myself back each time I wanted to reach for my truth. My neck is rosy from Indian burns of checking out the destiny that so eagerly awaits to emerge from my belly. My lips chapped from excuse after excuse because I let myself lack opinion and say so. Too cautious, I always thought my strength would break bones, and now I know.

I'll have to take accountability. I'll have to admit it. I thought I was doing the world a favor. Holding back and fighting off my inner demons by cutting off their air supply in the shape of "yes. Sure and why not's". Not knowing that my own well being was at stake. That my own well was running dry.

Can you see me? I need help. They say the spirit and self-love are the answer. Too often, they tell us why, but not every tactic can be applied. Some need encouragement, verbal reassurance and a pat on the back. Speaking what we don't see instead of lingering in disbelief. Some say, " don't trust your eyes and speak out loud" in order to drown out the noise from before. Others say, run from your problems because they aren't really there. Some say, dance the night away and each night with someone new.

But I say, slow down. Take your time. Write it out. Tell one friend, maybe two. Pray. Be honest and take baby steps, as many as you need. That might be what's best for you. Look at your wrists and loosen your grip. Feel the strength of your lips and medicate them with the truth within and let them heal. For every part of you makes up a worthy vessel. Every part of you deserves to heal.

# What Does Silence Do?

Silence has saved me from many things. Without much interaction, I enhanced my listening. With it, I was able to observe my outside world and see the differences in communication. What was appropriate and what required further questioning. Like why do people talk after they have already gotten their point across? Excessive expression to make up for time lost. Taking it out on others they are not connected to because this impression will last?

Why do we offer insults as compliments? That it means more to express discomfort than anything that made us satisfied. My mind often tries to make sense of what is and how we got this way. Why do we look down when we don't know something? That anything other than intelligence is somehow more appealing. That life shouldn't be lived this way. But isn't that how we grow? Admitting to what we don't know that way, makes room for more? I wonder, will we ever get to a place where silence is actually the go-to instead of spewing senseless words?

There is more emphasis on bridging the gap between

where we are and where we want to be. That moment of silence really is a lot of learning. Paying attention and the chance for proper application. It can show how much you care.

# Don't Give Up on Me

Don't give up on me. I haven't found the right words to say, so I'm left stunned until they come. It isn't easy. Being in my head all day. There, I always find the right words to say. But when the time comes to let it out, they seem to disobey me. I'm sorry. I don't want to waste your time, but I promise I can get it in time! If you don't give up on me. Show me that you care. Show me that you don't want to turn away at the site of my independent ways. I've been like this for so long, accustomed to what life has made me be. In order to protect myself. I know I don't have to protect myself from you but, I'm trying to change my view. Don't give up on me. Please. That's all I ask. I'll get there soon, no matter how difficult the task.

# What Can I Do?

Ambiguity is the blood brother to uncertainty. I can tell you that I'm here for you and that I'll never leave. But it's with that same potency in which you've left me. Alone with my own thoughts, my own fears, running around in circles of what went wrong and my desire to fix it. Mental gymnastics, twisting, turning topsy, turvy, my mind starts playing tricks on me. Secretly wishing, hoping and praying that with each sent text message, I could change your mind, a lyrical disease. That I can change. We could start over. Pose and take pictures as proof, so you see what I see.

"We look good together, don't we?"

Not knowing all this would breed a toxic seed.

Chains of internal rebellion because my soul knew better. I neglected my own self worth rejecting all the hard work it took to build up self-respect and bodily confidence. I never believed what I truly wanted. My lips sole duty was to laugh and tell jokes keeping the air between us light and easy. Not acknowledging that my true emotions were quite heavy.

Growing with intensity, waves found themselves crashing and breaking every levy. I was willing to reject my own heart because you expressed that you weren't ready. Time and time again, with each glance, you could have met me, but you chose to leave me empty. So, with time I walked away. I developed wounds and scars, and I could give them your name. Others would tell me I have every right to give you blame. But you gave it no attention, and it left me in shame. And for some time, I grew cold, and I let the distance grow between us. A plague of inactivity washing away what could have been. Stagnation.

A creation of what neither of us wanted, yet we allowed. And it killed me inside to leave it all behind because my heart was not built that way. So I prayed. I prayed that God would change the functions of my heart. I prayed he would change how deeply I loved. I prayed he would take these feelings away and remove the pain that my insecurities had caused. Yet nothing changed. Until I revised my approach.

I prayed God would love him as deeply as I always wanted to. I prayed that God would see him where he is and heal him from his shortcomings. I prayed for the strength to forgive him and the air between us to be restored. That even in our silence, it would communicate the truth. That I'll always love him no matter what we go through.

# The Separation

You could hear a pin drop. The silence in the room was deafening. So melodic, so majestic as we swayed back and forth. Anything could happen. Count to three, then a coin toss. Fate introduced by chance and at the mercy of someone else's hand, yet we remain unafraid. Instead, we wait in anticipation. The air which filled our lungs was infused with the purest of intentions. Wanting the best for us because who we are isn't who we'll always be. Growth. Change. Reaching new heights and reintroducing a new remedy to old pain. Maturation on new horizons. We aren't who we used to be. We wont always be the same. And I'll admit, that's what scares me.

You see, I was so used to the way things were before. Business as usual. Causal contradiction and walking time bombs. Ticking away, a kamikaze with eyelashes looking for her next victim. Pain personified in the way people would use you. They had done it so often it was probably something I had to get used to. Life had become plagiarised, and I felt I no longer knew the author. My rebellion had been televised. All eyes were on me and my actions compromised. I felt the need to perform for such a long time. A character on the stage of life. Yet life has a funny way of throwing things at you when you least expect it. A reminder that there's more in you. That such a reality is so wonderful and fearful that sometimes it can even scare you. Leaving you speechless at yourself, filling the room with such depth that you could hear a pin drop.

"I need more from you, and the world needs it too."

A call to action. Hustle sold separately, and adult assembly required. Going to the next level in life, there is so much is to be acquired. At every turn, I threw myself at my past because this new responsibility takes work and makes on real tired. Over and over, I wanted to go back to old ways, wanting badly for things to remain the same. However, I had to find it within myself to make amends with the things I couldn't change. Acceptance was the needed exchange. My life now needs what I have to release today. And I will. I guess that thing I have to start with is faith.

# Catching Up

Sometimes I feel left behind. That I was never taught how to say what I want. The strength of a voice is something I never knew for myself. That I wanted to say what was on my mind, but life punished me for speaking too loud. How it became impossible to get around. Getting used to maneuvering life without my mouth. I felt useless. I became best friends with pride. That with every external approach, I never let anyone else inside. It wasn't what I meant to do; I just felt left behind. And so the remedy became slapping doors and stomping my feet. I became desperate, so I relied on the noise outside to set me free. Not realizing people were repelling from me. And I'm sorry, I just felt left behind.

Others my age already knew what to say in order to get their way. I just wished things were different. That someone wouldn't give up on me and listen. That even if I didn't have the right words right away, I wouldn't be laughed at or dismissed. It hurts. All at once, the pain starts, and I'm left to mend my own heart. It's not easy. And now I've learned to drown out the need to express myself. It's not easy to deny yourself access to the internal remedy. What should I do? I only get older as I fall farther and farther behind. So I picked up a pen, and I started to write. Things that made sense that made me less tense. I wrote down all the anger and all the frustration. And the longer I wrote, the sooner I began to cry. Tears fell down my face. My pen ceased to write. I finally came face to face with me and what was finally happening.

I was falling behind with the world because I had to catch up with myself. I took too much time comparing myself instead of accepting myself. My changes, my emotional ranges. The things that prompted easier emotional exchanges. I'm sorry. I just felt left behind. But my job isn't to catch up to the pressures of the world. My job is to find out what's really true. What I found to be true is the love that surrounds me and you.

# Vulnerability

I never got the chance to tell you how much I loved you. That you really do mean the world to me. That with each passing moment, I don't want to sleep because my dreams aren't as wonderful as my reality. I never got the chance to tell you how much I loved you. That you were my favorite Grandma. The way you would call us over to give you some sugar in the most country way. How the wrinkle in your hands reminded me of the rivers that brought you here to California. The rivers you always told us carried the holy spirit that even lived within us. You'd call the quake "Rivers in your Belly".

I never got a chance to properly thank you. For raising me with as much love as you did. For sticking out the hard times no matter what it looked like. I'm glad that you stuck around. A girl always needs her dad around.

I never got a chance to help you the way I meant to. You always taught me independence and how to handle things on my own. But in doing so, I neglected the help that was needed at home. That I, too, had a part in helping you start, the other dreams that you too had in your heart. You always wanted to go back to school. How things have changed, and it's no longer easy like it used to be. I never got to say thank you for helping me. Mommy, you deserve all that you are striving for. You'll make it there. You'll get your degree and so much more.

I never got that chance. I always wanted one chance to tell you how I really felt. I know time has passed, and things aren't as easy as they were before. But I've grown up now. I can do things in a wiser way now. You should be proud. You've taught me the best way you knew how and today, I wear a crown. I'm not as cold as I once was. I'm learning to open up. I hope this can continue. Life has proven we only have so much time left. The truth is, there's strength in vulnerability.

# Not Again

It's happening again. All I've ever wanted to say sits right at the back of my throat. It's happening again. Where sweaty palms meet ruin as the opportunity to speak my mind fleets me. I'm overwhelmed. Not because I have little to say, but because I have so much. I've missed you. I love you, and I've always cared for you but, I'm stopped in my tracks. Is it pride? Or have I gotten my strength back? It's too easy now to leave it all on read and move on. Buried deep inside what I want to say because I'm not sure you'd hear it anyway.

It's happening again. My mind filling in the gap with assumptions. Like an acrobat, I jump to conclusion after confusion making record-breaking scores on the high beam. The gray area where we fill our communication has also offered the definition of our relationship status. We are now fond of "I don't know" and "I hate it here". It's not safe here. So I left. I never meant to, but it was the only way to be sane again. To get my strength back. It's happening again.

Making excuses for my behavior as if this is how I get

my true healing. It's happening again.

The thoughts I thought were so comforting, but instead, they were limiting beliefs. It's happening again.

My quiet place is no longer as happy a home as it once was. The solitude is deafening, and I can't hear the sound of true love, even if it faced me. So instead, it knocked. Waiting at the door of my heart to let it in. In my own time, in my own way, at my own pace. Slowly but surely, inching closer and closer, this warmth has filled my existence, shattering my core.

Wiping away every cobweb formed by stagnation and indecision. Smoothing out the crevices of unfulfilled promises and unhealthy expectations. I haven't opened up fully, yet I am changed. My hands no longer tremble from the solitude I placed myself in. My limbs are strong and can hold my body up with self-worth and God-given confidence. My eyes are open to see colors and embrace the beauty from within the things that I cannot change. Of the things that I wouldn't want to. My hair, my nose, eyes, lips and teeth. Everything about me. The closer I reach to open the door, I wouldn't want those things to change either. I accept them and just be. Although I am changing, I am overwhelmed. I've never let someone in like you before. Someone whom I've never seen yet, your presence is undeniable. It's finally happening. I am in awe for the first time in a long time. Atsomething new yet familiar.

Fresh and inviting, my eyes are opened to a new horizon, and it stretches to embrace me, nurture me and nurse me back to health. It's finally happening. I can see. Someone willing to see me through all of my ugly and unafraid of the hard work it takes to stay instead of leave. The power of creation lies in the palms of your hands, yet to be stepped down so I could know you better. It's finally happening. I'm amazed at who you are. That someone like you, with all power in his hand, chose the door of my heart and stand. Waiting for me to let you in.

With open arms, you rush in and embrace me. Drowning out the noise of my limiting beliefs and self-doubt, you strengthen me. Equipping me with wisdom to see the love the way it was always meant to be. Unwavering and loyal. That it doesn't boast or brag, insulting others and making them sad. Love is patient. Love is kind and strong enough to blow your mind. Indisputably potent yet gentle at the same time. I never thought it was possible for someone like me. Someone so far away hidden in the valley of disbelief. Leaving others on read as proof, I was a changed being. Thriving in relationship ambiguity, sitting in the highest seat offered by the scornful. My delight is no longer in what I thought but rather in what I know. It's truthfully happening. Consulting every measure before I act out of character.

It's happening. A change in how I approach life because hope has entered my space. It's happening. Optimism is a new friend that is far more energetic than I'm used to. But, I am balanced by the cool, calm and collected perseverance. Teaching me that things take time. It's finally happening. I want more out of life. The tides have shifted, and I want this for everyone. It all happens when you let love in.

# A Worthy Burden

Life tends to move so fast, sometimes I forget I have a say. That what I say actually matters, and will be taken into consideration one day. Some how, some way, I know that I can't always be everywhere at once. But I get there pretty fast with this cape and an M on my chest. I'm known to handle everything and keep things in place. Even after a long day, it still gets longer. Tending to the home is hard work. It is embedded in me to give my all to my family. Picking up the pieces others don't readily see. It's in my DNA how to perform a balancing act that caters to everyone's sanity.

I do it not because I have to but because I want to. I love you, and this is the best way I know how to show you. By giving up my dreams to build the dreams of my child. I longed to be more one day, and as I get older, things get harder. In spite of it all, I am encouraged that my time is now. This resolve won't leave my soul. Instead, it helps me to grow. For each stage of my life, there's a new way to behave. When the kids are grown and out there on their own, there's a desire to start new beginnings. Pick up the things that we put down for them. A chance to travel and see the world for all it can be. Picking up a new hobby and a chance to begin again. A worthy burden to bear. One where I wouldn't change a thing.

# Slow Down

Slow down. We must take heed and learn when we are taking on too much. Slow down. Practice being gentle with yourself. Take note of the things that make you uncomfortable. Are you not being heard? Are you being dismissed? Take a deep breath, and let it out. Take a deep breath, and let it out. It's not easy when you're so accustomed to the constant grind and shutting everything out. With it comes a hard exterior we know very little about.

Slow down. Calm your nerves. Anxiety is no true friend. It comes to raise your blood pressure and cut your breath short. It's time we noticed what happens to our bodies and practice what works. Self-motivation. The words that are readily spoken that we give to others should also be ready for yourself for the taking.

Clarification. Not trying to control every little thing that happens; it's not worth the aggravation. Such agitation isn't your portion and should not be mistaken. For reiteration, is not a friend of yours either. Simply put, slow down. We aren't done yet.

Take note of your trembling hands and inability to stand. Speak to each limb and cause them to have control again. That every quiver can no longer deliver the message that this condition is "uncontrollable" ever again. Take hold of your mind and do as the waves do. Sway back and forth and behold the beauty of the view. Go to a place that empowers you. Regaining your ability and being patient enough to see this process through. So start at the beginning and slow down. You go through a lot, more than what you let the world know. It's time you became gentler. You have so much more life to go.

# Don't Settle

One thing I know about settling is if you do so in one area, you do so in all other areas too. From your language to how you perceive life, they are all connected to what you believe you deserve. Don't settle. Because when you do, you tend to do so in all other areas too. Such as your career, maybe even in your love life. Not realizing that you become resentful of what's been placed in front of you when you do.

Unaware of how it makes you feel and what's going on inside you, there is a necessity to upgrade your perspective. It's not natural to stay stagnant and to demean what's important to you. Don't settle. Get to the root. Make a note of what can happen to you. In this place and in this state, you owe it to yourself to think straight. What do you truly want? What can you truly say? Those things can happen to you. If you believe they can today. Be patient and wait; it'll happen for you. It can happen today.

# Approach me

Approach me. Walking around, head held down, I'm blue. But, deep down, I'm hoping to be approached by you. The warmth of your encounter reminds me how much you love me. How much you care. How I thank you for simply being there. Keep on doing that. Keep on coming back. The ice-cold exterior I've surrounded myself in melts away at your warm gaze. I know it won't happen instantly; it may even extend beyond days. But, I promise you. Approach me; it'll help me heal from my pain. Before long we can create memories anew and together we can see better days.

# Stay

Don't give up on me. It's been such a long time since we've seen each other, but I haven't forgotten how much you mean to me. That with each passing moment, I can't forget your smile. How your warm words have impacted my lifestyle. Such grand notion through the commotion has really led me to be more open. You've taught me that life should be lived this way. Our inner demons should be brought to bay, and we have more power over them than we give ourselves credit. That we have a say. How these lessons mean so much, but I'll admit, it's been a while since I've opened up. Don't give up on me. I have the tendency to retract when a new threat attacks my mind. It's anxiety this time.

Shallow breathing and imaginations moving one hundred miles an hour. I haven't gotten a hold of them just yet. Don't give up on me. Trial and error is something I haven't grasped just yet. After all, it's been so long we haven't gotten a chance to see each other in a while. How bright you've always been even when you were a young child. How I longed to be just like you. From here, I learned from the perfect point of view. Underneath your wing, I took everything in. I held on tight, fastened my grasp for dear life as each moment flashed before my eyes. I am no longer a kid. I am learning more and more each day. But I haven't exercised my right to say what it is I'm feeling. What it is I'm dealing with. How I wish you wouldn't give up on me. I'm trying my best. I promise I am. I thank you for doing your best and giving all that you can.

# Still

I still love you. I always will. My actions may speak louder than my words. Well, they're supposed to. My heart, empty with regret. I can't stomach the thought of speaking just yet, because the pain will spew from my lips right away. I still love you. No matter how hard I try, each tear I cry can't make the pain go away. It's been months, no, decades, since I've had my way, and sometimes I wish it would all change. I still love you. No matter how much distance you place between us. No matter how many empty promises you toss my way, I know it's a ploy for me to say something different.

Each instance that pushes me further, I wanted to bring us closer, but it isn't time yet. You were still dealing with your own pain that I never knew. Processing loss and regret, your heart grew into what you don't even recognize. I'm sorry. I hope I didn't pass the chance to empathize. All I wanted was to pass the time doing what we both loved. Showing I still love you. I always will. I refused to be pushed off by the chill of your heart. I tried my best to help you find resolve by letting you vent and getting things off your chest. I'm sorry. That you never had a safe space to be yourself. But time doesn't have to be the blood brother to scarcity. The real truth is, you can have an abundance of time in its entirety. If you let it. We can start again. Remember that I still love you, and I always will. Never forget it.

# What Does it Mean to Heal?

What does it mean to heal? Why is it so important? Well, I've noticed it helps me to be more open. More open to life and new possibilities. How to get to this place, how to get to this view? Well, it isn't easy and can often take a lifetime. Sometimes, each layer can be peeled back with the help of people that's got your back. Taking time and precious attention to the wounds at hand. Noticing what hurts and being honest not to make things worse.

Slowing down time and taking a deep breath, picking up all the pieces and leaving nothing left. Utilizing the right remedies so that you can be restored back to health. Acceptance, forgiveness, affirmations, redemption and repetition. Doing it as often as necessary, a recommendation to feed your soul from your primary physician. Healing is a life long journey. It isn't easy. Something can be shed off in an instant, and others try to make the process hurry. But regardless, it's something we all need to do. Healing in itself is a necessity.

# The Tactics Against Me

Sometimes I can't blame anyone else. That self-sabotage got a hold on me. Once again, I've been pressured to do great things. Everyone else sees me a little differently. An overachiever, a star athlete, even prom court royalty. They don't know what goes through my head after the smoke clears. I'm left with the ways I alone see me. I am in the belief that the greatness I have can't reach its full potential. I only have this gift temporarily. There's pressure to be a master in my youth. That if I don't start now, I have no way of catching up. What's the use? I'll always be left behind.

"That's that, and that's my truth."

When that's not the truth at all.

I often say things I feel at the moment before I see the entirety of it all. I'm left to examine the world while I wallow in my feelings. I have a tendency to jump the gun and even say things I really don't mean. Sometimes, the only thing standing in my own way is me. I don't really mean to. I just know that

I feel so strongly about certain things sometimes. It tends to come out of my mouth each time. Every now and then, I remember that we have more power than we give ourselves credit. That's the power of manifesting.

Even though I want to vent and express my feelings, my world doesn't know the difference between a want and a need. So oftentimes, I need to be more careful about what I am settling in. My thoughts do more than make me question. What I have or what I am. I actually attract or retract well-deserved blessings. So for the right things to come, I need to take inventory of the thoughts that run through my mind. While only allowing constructive thoughts, the positive kind. The empowering things. It's about time that Self-sabotage no longer takes a hold on me and disrupts my seed. I want to be free. Now I believe that I finally can be.

# The Plea to Start Again

Create in me the tenacity to speak up and move forward. Create in me the ability to speak up and stand at attention like a soldier. To touch the world as I get older. To stop our warm world from getting any colder. To wake up early to a hot cup of folders. Bright and early create in me a fresh new wind. The nerve to let it all go and start again. To be happy again. This pain I no longer want to wallow in. Guard my heart as I embark on this new start. Starting with my confession and letting others in.

I know now that sometimes it happens from within. That resolve I've always been seeking. A ministry in itself that keeps on preaching. Debunking any validation I was seeking. Words of truth and words are proof. That the works of my hands would be blessed. That my steps are ordered in the right direction, and I take this time to make the right profession. That I am loved by the purest love that only you can give. Create me in security to trust what you've said about me instead of being fooled by what I see. Create in me the channel to find release. That what the world needs on the inside of me can finally be free. No, I don't see it now. I know it will take time. And as it does, be with me. By my side. In your presence, I will reside. In your embrace, I will hide. For the greatest work you want to do, starts inside.

# The Power of Silence

There's power in silence. A stand in the stillness that creates distance between meanings. What is, and what is meant to be. Silence is golden. Protection from being too open because oftentimes there's a battle in what's being spoken. A battle of the mind but warred with the mouth. If not careful, the wrong things can come out. Life and death are in the power of the tongue, and with the right words, the war can be won.

Silence can be used as a weapon of peace against violence. The most powerful way to say let life in and reduce the collateral damage. However, I know how people can be so dismissive in it. The assumption of your stance and how your heart can become a victim. I know the hurt. The pain in the distance. Without the proper amount of attention to it, it can be raw and quite cold. I'm sorry that silence has created a different mold. Sometimes it can be the catalyst to hold onto something old. Something happens. Deep inside. Sometimes you feel alone and cold. You tend to resent others because no one knows. I understand. That the feelings are there without the right words to share what's really going on. There's really something wrong. It can spread like a disease, a tasteless jelly.

Moving and touching everything in its path, proving to be quite sticky. It's sickly how it makes us, and I'm sorry. The reality of silence makes you feel like you feel it on your own. The house of your body is not really a home. While you are there, sometimes it takes time to let others near. However, I promise when you do, true warmth can come to you. Just by your actions alone, others can catch on. How to move and conduct themselves around you introducing a new song. A new tune of life no longer causing strife. There's sensitivity with your very life that others can catch onto. That doesn't have to leave you blue. Even when you've never said a word when people love you. Your worth is all the words that need to be heard. Never let anyone take away the power of silence that you possess. Don't fool yourself that in this state, there's nothing left. Be one with what's inside you. Such silence can give you vision and guide you.

# Meek Not Weak

I am meek, not weak. I know how to use my energy. That even though I am not as loud as you thought, it doesn't mean I can't hold my ground the way I ought. I am meek, not weak. I know exactly where to put my energy. I am aware that my response will not always be the same as you may want it to be. I am strong in my ability to carry on, regardless of how you see me. I am meek, not weak. I take time to see what others don't see. Attention to details and slow to speak. I know what works and what may not need approaching. I am intelligent in my speech. I am aware of my surroundings, and I think before I speak. I am meek, not weak.

I approach life differently. I let others go before me. I wait my turn, even when life tries to destroy me. I keep a happy disposition, but I am learning to voice my thoughts and stand by my opinion. I've had a hard time accepting this is how I do life. This is who I am. That my soft-spoken voice can actually slow time down and grab the attention of my fellow man. I have learned I don't have to yell to command the room. I don't have to be boisterous to make a man swoon. I don't have to yell at the clock to make it noon. I am, who I am and I will have my turn soon. Patience has been my secret weapon all my life, and it is the secret sauce to end all strife. I know who I am. I am meek, not weak. I know how to use my energy, I know how to impact any room. And with time, I can command the world soon.

# Young One

The need to be nurtured like the way mama always used to. The need to be caressed and cared for always lives on regardless of our age. The little boy or little girl we always grew up with will always be there. They will always need care. Whether it's a year from now or two, the young one on the inside will always need love too. They will always need the hugs we never got, the affirmations our elders forgot. They need the gifts and attention, love and affection. They also need to be held and a safe space to cry and feel their emotions out. The difference now is we must not place this burden on someone else or blame others for the sadness we once felt. We need to find a healthy outlet to ask for help. This hard work can start with self.

Mirror work.

Looking into your own eyes and speaking to your self-worth. Young one, I see you. You are not being heard, so I take the time to hear you out. Young one. You haven't been shown love so let me pour my love on you. Young one. You are greatness wrapped in an energetic ball, your energy bounces off the walls, and all you want to do is play. So let's take the time out and play. Young one. We can get our needs met and find balance. See, sometimes the little one on the inside us had a hard time growing up. They had needs that were never met and sometimes grew up to harbor regret. I never want the young one to have a stain and make a heavy heart. So it's time we took time for our young ones and take care of their heart. Show love to them little by little, and today you can make your start.

# What The World Wants

There is something that the world wants from you with your silence. The agreement and dismissal to take just about anything they give you. Whether a good fit or not, there's an expectation to fit everything into your schedule the way they want you to. Your silence communicates everything is alright when it may not be. It shows them that the say you have really doesn't matter. And that's not at all true. On the other hand, those that pay close attention know exactly what your silence is meant to do. It is meant to send a different message. That with each happening, you really are in awe at the audacity of people.

A movement and moment of disbelief that humans would treat each other this way. That we are all mistreated day to day. Unraveling the reasons things have been going on for this long. That the sadness like this itself is wrong. Your silence also communicates the resurrection of peace to a situation. There are too many opinions in one place, and we can't stand to judge what's going on. This is why they've brought to your face. Such madness we cannot erase. Such madness you choose to react against all with your silence. All without violence.

You walk around quiet but you're anything than just silent. It's apparent that whatever the world is trying to get from you, make sure they never get it. After all, they try to provoke the wrong things to prompt the wrong response. Stay silent. Use your voice for the right moments. This is the time you put the world on notice and use the right times to be outspoken. Your silence is a token ready to unlock the potential of a new way of living. All you have to do is see your silence differently. The world wants you to be silent forever, but use your silence as a weapon and stay clever.

# Enough

How do we know that enough is enough? We all have different dials and various gages. Ones that prompt us to come forth, and others to keep us in cages. What may set you off may not set off me. That with each passing moment, I'm picking up a lot, not just living vicariously. I needed some time away, some time to think. When enough is enough, and that's all that it'll be. I can't begin to express how many times I wanted to be free. That when I express myself, I hope you're the one listening. This hurt, this pain isn't all worth the suffering. Love shouldn't come with constant war. This back and forth, I can't take any more. Enough is enough.

While times are in constant changes, I don't know where the gauge is. How we treat our mother earth and put her babies in cages. This time without our involvement, she took the chance to heal herself. Enough is Enough. It's time we took better care of our time to be creative. What flows through us is enough for all ages. With each moment of growth, it can go through so many stages. How much depth there is once you take the time to turn the pages.

Enough is enough. It's time we gave more time to our elderly. For a time, they held us on their own backs with their hard work while the world cut them no slack. Enough is enough.

We have to pay them homage for all they have done. Finally expressing to them that it was because of their undying support that we finally won. Enough is enough. This is for all the times we never got through to the ones that didn't care. Enough is enough. It's time to finally take that chance to share what was always there. Enough is enough. It's time to reach for those who we are called to trust and get out of our own heads thinking it's just "us". It's time to step up. Because enough is enough.

# CHAPTER 2
# WHISPER

Whispers are indications of soft expression. Often, one speaks in a whisper to not disrupt what is already happening in the air. As other messages are being passed, a whisper can go unnoticed or unaccepted. We fail to recognize the effort it took to carry the whisper and the risk along with it. Battling inner demons with the desire to push takes precious time and sensitivity. Sometimes breaking through pride and evading embarrassment, a whisper still yearns to be heard. In this section, such poems have been written from the process of breaking one's shell.

Describing the tough exterior that was there previously and finally broke, even if only a little bit. How it does something very important for one's heart and mind to reach this level of expression. The breakthrough of finally finding release. How it's just the start of a process worth enduring. Tackling the areas of love, following one's dreams and even qualifying one's space, this section is meant to give an approach to the things that have been previously dismissed. Allow the strength that was once known to come back and show up with these poems. And find yourself there. Give yourself permission to arrive at a whisper, even if it's hard.

# The Process

Take a deep breath. Close your eyes. In and out. And with each breath have one word in mind. Anxiety. Depression. Sadness. Wrath.

Leave. You are no friend of mine. Continue.

Lack. Depression. Guilt. Fear. Leave. There's no room for you here. Shame. Pointing the finger. Blame. Accepting derogatory terms other than your God-given name.

Leave. It's time to go your stay has been too long.

Disease. Brokenness. Comparison and put down. I will no longer wear your colors. I will no longer be your clown. It's time to give up my rags in exchange for a crown.

My God! I gave too much voice to the wrong choice. I gave in to the fear and believed all the noise. My God, be with me. As I take a deep breath and close my eyes. You are there. I'll admit that I'm scared. I've never thrown my crutches to the floor before.

I've never walked on my own and opened the door. Letting go of what I once knew before. But no matter, I acknowledge your sovereignty now as you sit high on your throne. You are near. I'm never alone. This void that I feel, I had over in an instant but be with me. Because I fear this will be easy to revisit.

Take a deep breath. Close your eyelids. Fall into grace. Because the past can be easy to chase. A world of familiarity, a world we already know. But to lay hold of who we are, we must stand firm and let go. So it makes it easier to grow.

# Patience

Slowly but surely, things take time. You can do things your way, or you can do them with time. Arm in arm, hand in hand, even things in the air must one day land. Time holds a precious place in our lives, and with it, can make us strong. We can do so in more ways than one. Being able to wait things out and work against our own habits can help us find out what's really going on. Beneath the surface, we may be dealing with a reality that we sometimes don't want to face, including some toxic habits that we need to break. Impulsive desires and reactions of wanting things our way right then and there, no questions asked.

When life doesn't always work that way. Things take time. Especially the things that can change your life. The time for relationships to grow and thrive. The time for an idea to grow and thrive. It also takes time to deal with people too. Getting to know their wants, their desires and needs. That what works for one may not work for another, and patience teaches us that this is ok. That everyone learns at their own pace. Not everything in life is a race. Or getting to the next stage. It's Ludacris, to think that your life and someone's will always go the same way. Your journey is not theirs, and theirs is not yours. This life is tailor-made to bring out what is on the inside of you. The greatness that can only come out with patience itself.

Who's missing who?

What would you say if I told you your dreams were missing you?

How they missed how often you pursued them. That they didn't want to merely lie with you when you slept, but instead meet you when you woke.

That your pursuit was so full of zest and zeal as they drew closer and closer each day. That they were within arms' reach as you called their name until you stopped! They were right there, but you stopped.

Why did you stop? Why couldn't you hold on for just a few more moments? After all, you were walking down the aisle. Getting prepared to unite as one. Seamlessly intertwining yourselves together so much so that no one could tell where you ended, and they began. All it took was a simple yes. For when you are that bold and that in love with destiny, the universe has no choice but to forever hold its peace.
What would you say if I told you your dreams were

waiting on you? What could you say then, when all they wanted was to be with you and make every day worth living? That to experience them was not a temporary escape but rather an everlasting refuge. What would you say then if I told you their very existence was depending on you?

In order to allow them to breathe day in and day out longing to be held by you because they were on their way. They were arriving in the nick of time. That these very dreams were not sent by your own doing but rather someone else's. What if your mother sent for them? And what if your great-grandmother made room for them? What if they spoke utterances in the nighttime and searched the night skies all these years so one day, they would someday be your reality? That your dreams would meet you face to face. An occurrence of the ages.

Carried out by generations. The event of the century, if only you truly knew.

What would you say if I told you that your dreams were shunned by you? Not by the world, not by this controversial pit we call humanity. Not by this leviathan we blame to take the blame off of ourselves. What if I told you that the very language you spoke could either give life or bring forth the knife? Can you really fathom how strong you have become in your disbelief?

Do you truly know how powerful you truly are?

I pray the pit you find yourself will soon bring you deliverance. I pray for the time you find the light liberating you from what is now that you are prompted to do something about it.

I pray you miss your dreams, more than they miss you.

# Frequency

Vibrations, frequencies, frequently letting me know where I should be and should not be:

That what you give off directly affects me. Your speech, your tone, your overall energy.

All reaching out to grab me. Asking for the company of me.

I'd have to ask initially, "are you filled with synergy or toxicity?"

"Empathy or Calamity?"

Heartfelt, notion or sadness and senseless commotion, see I'm cautious now.

Finding more and more that where I am is not where I'm meant to be.

It takes being sharp to change direction so soon.

That charting the waters now will do me a disservice

because the tide is coming in soon.

The winds of change are among us. Are you ready? Because we have no time to waste.

We need to follow the same vibrations. We need to be on the same frequency.

# Holding Hands is Dangerous

I'm telling you that the dangers of holding hands are detrimental to my survival and do something to my vital. It's the killer, mediocre, evidence of being halfway up the mountain, undeniable proof that we are off the ground but nowhere near the top.

In fact, the culprit is stealing what my soul has to offer because the roots run that deep.

The curse of pounding hearts and sweaty palms. See, holding hands robs me of the depths of my being yet speaks to the simplicity of my innocence.

Offering sweet, simple bliss and the nerves kicking in after, no during our first kiss.

Look, holding hands is melodic. Asking for your hand in mine, wondering if we should swing back and forth while we walk. Or wondering if our swing's momentum could cut the wind and it'd be too loud, so we should keep quiet and not even talk. Only to hear our hearts heave by how nervous we are 'cus I've managed to get this close to you and nothing has gone wrong.

Holding hands is dangerous, better yet detrimental and does something to my mental like, are we even doing it right? Am I holding you too tight? Are we too close? Is this the right perfume you like? Are we swinging too fast? Are we pacing our steps just right? Holding hands is dangerous, better yet detrimental and does something to my mental.

Like, I want you to squeeze me tight but at the same time be gentle.

Like, I want to feel the strength of your palms and intertwine your fingers with mine. But then I don't want to get all sweaty, 'cus if I let you go to wipe mine dry, then I risk your warmth leaving me already. I'm telling you, holding hands is dangerous and proving to be detrimental because I promise you it does something to my mental. I wish this was the easy part, how can this be so hard? After all, we just finished walking barefoot on the sand, and now we're at my car.

After all, we just finished dancing, jiving to our silent yet vibrant heartbeat, and you've made it to my immediate memory. I may have forgotten what you've said verbatim but, you've achieved the stamp of approval with my circadian rhythm. You've latched onto my motive, locomotives and private notions only God has descended, written down and offered notes and…

Yet, we still can't seem to find resolve.

I still need coaching.

My naked still needs clothing.

'Cus I've gone my whole life noticing that holding hands is dangerous, better yet detrimental. But I'll admit, I'm overcoming what it does to my mental.

# Fewer Words

Lately, I've got fewer things to say. With too many thoughts and ideas clouding my mind and lengthening my days, I'm addicted. Addicted to the solitude that peace gives me.

Welcoming me with open arms, I'm wounded by my decisions of being "busy".

Not productive, not progressive, not conducive to society in any way. Just dizzy.

Turning flips and engaging in lyrical gymnastics, how I'm still sane through it all, is shy from fantastic. Often we become supreme fanatics of our own imaginations. Prisoners of self-gain, worshiping our pain, it's a crutch. And to think, taking just one self-care day a month is coming in clutch? Only to get so worked up, over and over again, to end up in the same rut. No wonder our streets are running amuck, with people who don't know when to give up,
all their problems....
all their struggles....
all their troubles ...and simply look up.

Lately, I've got fewer things to say because there's an emphasis on what I need to hear in this season. Things are becoming more familiar and more potent in their place in my life for familiar reasons. I was clouded, jaded and surrounded by the fog that found itself deep. The stones weren't nearly as rough yet, in my body, I keep each encounter safe with cuts and bruises alike. I'm exhausted.

So, I lick my wounds in private. I duck off and observe those I want to keep at an arm's distance because now, then, I make it harder to become your target. However, in actuality, you have the power to change my entire reality. I know that now, but I still build a wall. Evidently, I stand unsteady and unready for my future to change. Unsure and unclear of the mold it will take. Its shape is predestined, but my present isn't the gift I thought it would be. It's wrapped up, covered up from the world and often, it's even hidden from me. The truth is, it's prompting me to give up,

All my worries…
All my anxieties…
All my questions….and simply look up.

Lately, I've got fewer things to say because of my overwhelming terrors of being alone. My addiction to be strong, my anxieties of being wrong, soon to be reminded they were all nailed to the cross and laid at His throne. The storm in which I found myself have all been calmed, and the thunder clouds have ceased along with the tides that promised to swallow me whole. In the midst of it all, He found me and offered me His hand. A promise to cover me when my heart grew cold and to hold me when I couldn't stand. An ear to hear even when I didn't have all the words to say. The tears that roll down my face, the liquid prayers and praises that go up releasing.

All my sadness…
All my fear….
All my pain…...because I simply looked up.

# Boundaries

It's funny. I never took myself seriously before. Laughing and passing jokes, I easily made light of things. The air around me was easy for things to come and go. I just didn't know it set the stage for people to do so also. People calling themselves my best friend, and before long over something dumb happened, and the relationship would end. Not worth it, not worthy of the commotion, I paid it no mind. I buried the offense in time and went on with my day. I continued to laugh and even started to pray. Confession and reflection I was weightless as I roamed the city. I catered to myself and external health; I found what made me feel pretty. Long nails and eyelash extensions while the neo-soul was buried beneath. In grief because the pain I experienced in my childhood had not yet found release. Isn't it funny? I never took myself seriously before?

I thought that to do so, I needed to enter the corporate world. Wear a pinstriped suit and make more money than I ever had before. That a fat check would keep in check my mind and focus away from the things that no longer mattered. Consisting of who left and those who wouldn't bother to stay. Revenge in silence and nose in the air. No one can touch me here. In the clouds, I was untouchable until reality set in. I was all alone up there.

Taking flight is always the easy part, but bringing others with you… that's where the true journey starts. I never took myself seriously before. What it meant to me to be near me. I never exercised setting healthy boundaries. Maybe that's why it made it easy for things and people to come and go. The hurt I felt, I thought they'd know. I never took myself seriously before.

I never took the time to know what made my heart sore. What took more time to heal now than before. That words do hurt like bricks and stone. Sometimes those closest to you have a better aim to throw them. We must take ourselves more seriously now.

We can feel life and death more easily if we are not careful. Manifestation in God's most worthy creation. We are powerful beyond measure. I still don't understand how causing pain to bring some pleasure? It's no longer funny that I didn't take myself seriously. That I took hurt far easier than I took love. And I'm sorry to my own body. Please forgive me. I never knew how to lay healthy boundaries, and now I want to because I now know the importance of keeping you safe. Keeping us safe. The importance of exercising my right to have a say. In what goes and what doesn't. I want the comfort of standing up for myself. It starts one step at a time. One chance and one opportunity at a glance, I am searching for my strength. I am searching out my outlet. I now seek wisdom amid council. As you offer your help, I can find my truest self. One worhty of love and worthy of being respected.

# Whisper

What is it about a whisper that makes me forget I am here? Is it the message, or the mere fact one has to listen with their heart and not just their ears? I barely enter the room, yet I am still here. A message carried by the wind I'm hoping someone would let me in. But even I forget where I am. Due to the potency of a weep, any other intensity seems wrong. That anything not boisterous or loud must not be very strong. That the cadence of a whisper cannot be heard unless it's in a song. That, although I wasn't heard, it doesn't mean I wasn't talking all along. I'm learning that a whisper is heard by those destined to hear it. A secret straight from God, an answer to the cause, a cheat code to the mess we've found ourselves in. Can only be learned if we drown out all the noise and lean in.

Soft-spoken and meek with my lips, I am still a force to be reckoned with. Fastened with what matters most, a host of many wise words packaged in the form of a lamb. I am what I am. But I'm learning to love every bit of her as best as I can. That her sweet disposition on life can stop a war from happening.

She can bridge the gap of understating with her open ears and open palms, ready to receive the gift you've wrapped in frustration. She is not afraid of your strength because she knows it comes in so many sizes. She's not afraid of the forms. Because she knows that soon healing will come. Even in the form of a whisper. Because it's in this, the answer such a remedy can be delivered. And yes, a whisper can sometimes make me forget where I am. However, it reminds me not of what I can do but what the Lord can.

# It's Not Easy

I see you. You do reps until it hurts. You bench press your pain. You do crunches to kill your abs, hoping to kill your depression too. You do bicep curls to avoid curling up into the corner of your room because you know anxiety has a way of stopping you in your tracks. So you attack the track. Dominating hurdles, evading the devil as you take back all he tried to steal from you. And as you pass the baton, you press on to winning the race. But sometimes, your feet aren't as fast as your tears. So while you run, they run, bringing to mind your fears. Reminding you, you've gotten this far. But there's still such a long way to go.

# Range of Emotion

We are wonderful human beings. Simply complex, and in our complexity, it is compelling how much we change. So many ranges we can express on a daily in so many ways. Various notions explain such compassion. How we love and how it proves to be everlasting. What we go through to get it without even asking. We have proven to be sacrificial. That which we put ourselves on the line for is worth sacrificing. And it's a wonderful range of emotion. It takes so much in you to be so open. Being able to articulate and own them all, it's baffling how one can battle while feeling so small.

I can't imagine that all you go through really challenges you in ways I couldn't believe. But what I can say is that we have the right to feel them all regardless of who's asking. Happiness, joy, rage and depression. All are emotions that we feel regardless of what's being spoken. I wonder if we can get to a place to fully accept them. Own them all and give ourselves permission not to feel so small. That if the natural response is to cry, not feeling bad about that at all. Instead, owning every tear that falls. It takes some opening up, not to others but to yourself. Have you allowed yourself permission to just be regardless of who sees? I'll admit this, you may have to slowly. That when each emotions arises, you must take the time to identify the why? What is going on, and what is in the root that lies. And being honest. Not sugarcoating but being gentle. For we are wonderful human beings, simply complex. And we should own every part of ourselves regardless of what comes next.

# Growth

I know what's happening.

It is an unfamiliar feeling. That what you're finally getting out, has an aftermath feeling. These thoughts are racing through you're head and seem to get lost in what is being said. It's true, it's a fact. Instead of regressing, you're changing. I've always wanted this for you. It's weird, sure. Noticing all the odd happenings that lead to being mature. Leaving things in the wind, addressing things from within, finding a different angle to things, and making your application.

Making amends with what was and what is. That you're finally noticing what true growth is. To stand in the face of adversity and not give in. Running at the hard conversation and not resist the tension. The knowledge that you've acquired over this past time is now something that can help you shine. I know getting there isn't easy, and you aren't going it alone. Everyone has their season, and everyone exercises what they are shown. We've got to be careful with such growth because it challenges who we are and challenges what we know. It is also a harsh reality that the more you grow, please note. Where you are headed, not everyone will go.

# How to Handle Disappointments

I never thought I'd be here, in this place, in this space. Doing life this way. I never thought I'd endure such heartache. I thought the pain would never go away. That as I sat with my thoughts, replaying what took place, over and over again. You fell short again. You were late and rarely showed up again. I thought You forgot about me. I thought you forgot about me. These feelings replayed and replayed, and soon they were the wood I used to build a fence around my heart. At this point, I was all out of second and third chances. I was all worn out of broken promises. My tender heart couldn't take it. I was ready to trade it in for a new one. That is until one day I saw you come home late.

Full uniform with a large but heavy smile on your face. You were relieved to walk through that door once again. You walked slow, yet you hugged me close. The way a dad hugs his daughter, this is the hug I know. Ready to unwind from the way, my emotions melt away, and at this moment, I found grace. As you get older, you are doing life the best way you know how by breaking your back and providing for us by the sweat of your brow. And you've done it without question for years. You've held it all in. I don't know if you shed any tears. You don't ask for a pity party. You don't ask for anything in return.

You ask me about my day and play board games that require us to take turns. You are doing your best, and you're human. You're getting older, so we must be gentler with our elders. I know this so much more now, and I hold it dear. Any disappointments I held against you, I let it go with the wind. I can't live life anymore, harboring the past in. I had to let go to fully enjoy the present that we are in. And I thank you for everything you've always done. I don't know what I'd do without you. Thank you for doing the best you could and being my best friend.

# Choices and Assumptions

The most powerful thing God has ever given us is the ability to choose. Choosing what we want out of life and how much we put into it. Whether or not we want to stay grounded in what we are living in or quitting altogether. The worst thing you can do is try and take that away from them by making an assumption. Assuming something that may or may not be true. Working against the truth assumption fills in the gap with the creativity that imaginations use.

What you "think" may or may not be true. It isn't something I'd advise we always do. An assumption takes away your ability to choose and your ability to grow. Old ways aren't always the way to handle you because, believe it or not, we are changing every day. That we are adding some new things and taking others away. Making adjustments and using new ways to take on the battles of life. It is a choice we can make with each passing moment. An assumption takes that away. And I can't stress this enough, we owe it o ourselves to allow the growth for someone else. You are allowed to make choices, and I'll never take that away. I'm learning to work against my assumptions and ask away.

# Be a Bridge

Be a willing vessel. Bridge the gap between generations to bring understanding. We lack that these days. The way to connect without disarray. Doing so without judgment, I've always wanted to see life your way. How everything seemed to be so much simpler, and people had fewer worries. There was no rush to constantly be in a hurry. Things slowed down. The vision wasn't so blurry. There were tall tales and funny stories you told your kids in order to paint a bigger picture. Where metaphors and similes were the norms. With your language, you painted a pretty picture. Now there are so many changes, and the messages get distorted somehow.

The youth has turned their focus on pop culture and what gets the most views. We have done so much, and this has distorted the view on what's happening in our present. That there is a disconnect between generations, and no one is willing to fill in the gap of understanding. Why aren't we patient enough to see what they see? That we should spread more love than the violence we keep offering. That time isn't fleeing from anymore and we need to take time to do the

right things. That the responsibility of bridging the
gap

# Worth It

You are worth it. Of all the great things in life to come your way. I know things haven't always been easy. And sometimes things aren't the way we thought they'd be. You're still worth it. That what you have the world needs to the highest degree. You're worth it. That sometimes, we can't make it on our own. Those are the times we need some encouragement. Don't worry, you're worth it. That as time goes on, your purpose gets moved to the back seat because other things need your attention. Bill, health, taking care of ill family are only a few things to mention.

That just because other things leave you drained, you still have purpose in your veins, and you're worth it. You're still worth it. Of the right kind of love to start again. One that is pure and doesn't have to be bred in so much pain. A love that introduces peace and promises to learn all about who you are. A love that doesn't force anything that isn't already there. A love this isn't skeptical and doesn't breed fear. You're worth it. A thousand times over. And soon the world will respect that, a wonder to be discovered.

# Make it Last

The feelings that I love feeling are ones I never thought I'd accompany with healing. That it would be therapeutic to fall asleep to the sound of your voice. That things would fall into place after making such a great choice. I decided that my job was never to do anything or say anything that wasn't authentically me. I found in my life this far is to just be. Be happy, be sad, be mad, be glad. Be good to those that love me and be good to myself. For life has an expiration date, and there is a current we can choose to make.

The ability to join in or be the answer allows you to develop your character and choose faith. Finally, deepening the love that is meant to last. It dawned on me. The feelings that I love feeling. I've decided I wanted them to last. They offer the most healing. Being able to set an atmosphere of peace in my own space and bask. With eyes closed and head tilted back, I light a candle and draw a bath. These are the moments I want to last. Other moments are worthwhile too. A stroll in freshly cut grass far away from the city. Small flowers growing up tall and blooming so pretty. A breeze that carries away any and all insecurities leaving me empty. Empty of what I don't need and taking away what cannot stay.

## CHAPTER 3
# TABLE TALK

Right about now, it's time we talked out loud. Table talk is the chance to hear yourself and own what is being said among others. We are free and can do a lot with what we know. We are coming to realize the hurt and that pain that life has caused us, and we are not afraid to let others know. We are not afraid of the changes that happen within ourselves, but we also give that freedom to someone else. In this section such poems have gotten a little more personal. Coming toe to toe with changes and having to openly forgive others who have wronged us and tactics on doing so.

These opens are meant to open up to what has taken place objectively while releasing blame and whatever offense that has tried to hold people in a certain place in our lives. That things like trust and time itself play a huge factor in giving yourself permission to be great. That it is ok to start moving in a confession of what was, what is, and what you want to take place in life. With table talk, start to open up with a reality that invites change. And it's ok to share these things with other people. No more holding it in. Let the emotions win. Let growth in.

# What is Time?

Seasons are like time. Holding each other by the hand, introducing shadows as the sun sets on the highest mountain offering its well-kept hallelujah. A promise as the birds chirp while taking their turn, adding to the choir of praise, I often wonder if time would ever add to my peace. See, I never told anyone this, but time always seems to escape me. And I wonder if whether or not those hands would reach out to hold me and protect me from myself.

I have the tendency to keep busy.

With each passing moment filling up my own space task after task, one by one, bit by bit, I am amused at a new beginning. Just like January. Just like Springtime. A fresh wind covers the horizon, and the grass is greener than it has been previously. The scenery is fonder in the countryside compared to the city. The birds are louder now. The sun brighter now. But time is faster, how? Why wont it stop? Am I the only one who feels this way? Am I the only one who craves true peace? If I make this confession, will they look at me funny? Say I must be sick and prescribe me with tea and honey. Point me to the world outside, cus' in Cali, it's always sunny. Or maybe a break from the city, book a flight to the country? Change my scenery. But I am old enough to know, change cannot merely be external; it must come from within me. The main culprit is my anxiety. Holding me hostage and kept me from moving forward with reminders of what went wrong. My past. My mistakes. My shortcomings. Ashes upon ashes, burns and boils from metal plates I want to escape, but how? Time escapes me.

The poison and potion, I no longer want stagnation to be my portion. I want freedom from the shackles. So, I make my confession. I slow down my breathing, and I lighten my load. I let go. I must admit to myself, it was too much for me to carry to begin with. I can no longer do it, not all on my own. And with time, I learned that's ok. Healing is a necessity. Making one with the past, articles of an hourglass, time is not my enemy. For with her, I learned a lot. What is true peace is, and what it is not. Looking at her in with the lenses of abundance instead of scarcity. And the truth is everything has its season, and seasons are like time.

Holding each other introducing the breeze in between palm trees, there's a true paradise in release. A promise that I am not alone and I don't have to be a victim to the struggle in order to feel significant. That being held together is not a product of the hands of time but rather the companionship of patience with myself. Working as one, letting her have her perfect work and chiseling me like a diamond. Worth it to endure, we are destined to shine. Move at your own pace, and know that nothing you go through goes to waste. Each moment has its season, and seasons are just like time.

# The Signs

How much do we ignore, how much do we miss? That there were signs this whole time that we often dismissed. Amid life, some things tell us to "stay away" or warning us "not to engage". Often times we are notified that we need to clear the stage. Of who no longer is serving us now like it did before. What have we done? We've missed out on so much by being in the wrong place. That where we are now is dealing with now is not the proper case. That we should be further along in life and that we need to change course. I can assure you that sometimes we can think on these things but we aren't supposed to stay here. That we have to be renewed in our minds about what we've done. That it wasn't time wasted but rather time spent. And it can be redeemed as long as we spend time doing the right things. Looking for our purpose. Starts first by paying attention to the desire in our hearts. That there's trouble in the world, and we carry the answer. Such an answer is something we can bring with our very lives when done right. It's time we start taking the time. It's time we started paying attention to the signs.

# The Truth About Belief

If you don't believe, the deficit is definite. That without this key ingredient, there's only so much that you're left to deal with. That anything we try to achieve is really not all that it's cracked up to be unless there's something that grounds us and gives our life true meaning. That its easiest to want less, do less and let life take its course randomly. Senselessly wandering. Aimlessly aiming and constantly waiting. Waiting for the right thing to happen and the next thing to come around. And if it doesn't, it can be quite easy to throw it all to the ground. But there's a promise that we can always rely on.

That in this newfound freedom we can always call on. We can finally do away with all that tries to keep us down. So if we believe the opposite is true, there's so much in the world that we are destined to get through. But I bet you're wondering, "what is it about the belief that got you through? Why do we need it, and what does it do?" It got me through almost losing my only shot at higher education. After my first year, I almost lost it because it was the first time I had ever wandered so far. Belief got me my first car. That if I would save, handle business and focus on my studies, I finally made room for gifts to enter into my life. My new home. Without a job or even bank statements to clear my name, I could make do with a new gain. Looking back, all of these things were impossible. That I would have never thought I'd get through such close calls over and over again. But I know that belief itself in God really helped paved the way. He really saved the day.

# Trust

Trust is a terrible thing to break because it is terribly hard to make. Out of nowhere, we expect something to build our relationship on. A strong foundation with little expectation that you pass up the chance to treat me wrong. Otherwise, I'll write it in a song. Then I'll be a millionaire before long, and it's funny. I should be thanking you. You taught me what trusting someone feels like.

How safe it may have been, but I realize it may never be the same again. This time I'll be smarter. This time I'll love harder. And this time, I won't punish you for the relationship I have with my father. That even though we can't seem to get it together, there's no reason for us to grow farther. So trust me, and I'll trust you. That way, we can learn together the true power of what the right love can do.

# What It Takes

Some say you gotta' heal, but can't instruct you on how. Saying "change your shoes," but they ain't walked with you for a mile. It's funny how we lay down the process for you to follow, prescriptions of pills and potions for you to swallow. Tell you to wash your windows so you can see clearer, but they don't see how many times you've cried in the mirror. What we don't mention is how much distance is created. Allegation and instructions there's clearly a lack of intimacy. And It baffles me. People will have their opinions, but the bulk of my process involves you. I need someone to talk to. I've never been safe before. The finger has always been pointed at those with a mental disease. Not knowing they have been diagnosed just like me. So sometimes I medicate with trees, and that's so unlike me. I used to be the one so unlikely to follow the trends of society. Help me. Deep down, this is a false peace, yet I'm fooled by its temporary.

They say you gotta' heal but don't tell you how. Instead, tobacco companies advertise "your need for this" while preying on an innocent child. So I try. I take a step in the deep end, hoping you'll jump in and save me. And you did. And I thank you for it. I didn't make it easy. I rebelled. I screamed, and I yelled. I put up a fight and built walls to spite you. The fact that you were in authority, I tried to wear you down and bring you fatigue. Over time, the one truly tired was me. Tired of putting up a defense, thinking I didn't need saving. Because at sixteen, the world tries to feed you everything. And it's truly overwhelming.

So they try to help you heal, and they tell you to try a whole lot of things. Some of them work, and others aren't meant for you. Each with their own tactics and internal processing. I've learned to be ok with what works for me. I work out. Sometimes I run or do a little boxing. Taking out my aggression in a positive and competitive space. After I run and blow off some steam, I take a shower and rest my eyelids. I have more awareness than I did before. I gain more clarity, and I remember this calms my nerves, and my road to healing is better than before.

They try to suggest things that will help you heal. I had to find out for myself what works for me. Trial and error are sometimes the "how". Learning how much I can maintain even in the now.

# Starting Over

There are times where we've had to take an honest assessment of what happened. That not everything that went on the way we wanted them to. That we might have said some things we didn't mean. Or done things we wish we could just take back. It is important to know that to properly heal, we must accept the facts. That these things happened. We cannot make them go away, nor can they be erased. And although this is something we cant do, this is something we don't have to.

That there is a possibility to start a new. Fresh and in a new point of view. Starting from where we are and in a new set of shoes. That this mile we can walk can make us brand new. A fresh wind is available to you. It's not easy to leave things behind because they mean so very much. But it's so sad to me that we can't do anything with a barren touch. That some things no longer matter the way they used to, and that's ok. In starting over, we have a second chance. Things can be done right by you. You can start that business you've always wanted to try. You can write that book that you've always kept inside.

It's available to you. And it can be something new for you to discover. Make note that this treasure is worth starting over.

# Permission

I haven't had permission to feel before. That I was destined to be strong always. My bloodline held bones of marrow and blood of crimson destined to be cold like the rivers we crossed for freedom. Free in my body, but what about emotionally? I was never given permission to properly release. That my problems were mine and mine only. No one else cared about me. That I ran out of time, and each emotion expired and was no longer mine. Crying was reserved for the babes and for the weak. Sensitivity left me as a teenager and was replaced with competition and comparison. Vanity passed as sanity because I couldn't call myself worthy of any attention I'd get from the opposite sex without it. Building walls around my heart because it was more important to perform than to process. A product of the projects. Yet this defect affects our entire nation.

I never got permission to feel before. Others around me needed my mental capacity. I had developed the ability to sift through emotion and had applied a simple yet complex construct. Objectivity over subjectivity. Fact over feeling. What's actually happening over what I thought I was seeing. And it worked for a long time. Skating through circumstance after situation, making my mistakes, and helping others with theirs, I'm the strong one after all. Offering advice, I myself don't take it because I would never be in that situation. Right? Instead, I found myself with a new scenario. Bags and bags of experiences piling on each other in the form of childhood trauma, depression, abandonment, and attachment issues. All aching to be dealt with, but instead, I ran it off at the gym. Any time I had the chance to share, I'd let no one in.

I never gave myself permission to feel. It was safer this way. The distance I created formed an obstructed view. Painting a picture with a different hue. Strong and my problems, few. But that was as far as I knew. The stain on my heart grew until it festered into what seemed like an incurable disease. That I never got the chance to feel. So I tried it for the first time. Bit by bit with each tear. I found release, so I wrote. Harmonizing with my pain, a new note introducing hope. That what I felt was valid. That each emotion, candid were mine to be owned and not to be wrongfully handled. So I cried. I got angry. I let the frustration breed reason. Recognizing I was hiding behind smiles to keep oppressors close. That them cracking jokes on me would create tough skin and strong bones, not knowing it would create trauma later on. I felt it all. And it was time to give myself permission not just to feel but to finally heal. But what does that look like? Some argue it's time to be strong like my ancestors, raise it up and fight! Others say let pride arise and keep the offense inside. Utilizing mind games for them to figure out new approaches to try. But true healing is none of the sorts. Its a righteous man's sport to forgive and let go. Acknowledge the pain, and you write down their name. One by one naming the offense but not handing out blame. Recognizing what you had control over and knowing the difference in what you cant change. This is true strength. A muscle to be worked. A decision to let go of the hurt. Give yourself permission. It will cure any disease. And with time, it will teach your generation the life of ease.

# Validation

I love me, but I need to hear you say it too. That it does something in the back of my mind, I bet you never knew. That builds me up on the inside. That it prompts me to be free and move swiftly across the room. With heads held high, how it does something to the mind when you know you are seen. Carrying motive becoming more open what's a compliment if its not spoken? And some people take this way out of proportion. Some need it time and time again or else they think those in love are joking.

Validation in its prime has done something to our minds. That we can't move forward unless it's given all the time. When did we place more emphasis on external love? That without it, our world goes black and that if we don't get it when we want it, we'll never get it back. How sad is that? To place emphasis on bracelets and gifts aplenty when the compliment itself may be empty. When  did validation become so necessary? When did we replace the emphasis on our outside world instead of the world within? That it mattered more if it came from you instead of me. Now there's nothing wrong with a compliment;

there's just something wrong when that's the basis of where we define qualification. For just about anything in life, we will face trials. Ups and downs that will cause one to frown.

Beyond imagination and beyond definition, things will tend to weigh you down. It's in these moments that we shouldn't rely solely on those to place the crown we already have on. That when a door closes, that's the indication there's one for you that's wide open. No one can shut what is destined for you, no matter the opportunity. And so it's so important that the our attention is filled with the right affirmations. Validation. Doesn't have to be the thing we seek that, in turn, leaves us broken. Validation. Is something you don't need from anyone else regardless if they stay or leave. Validation. Can rob you of the true power you have, so make sure you speak. Speak into your life what you want to see. Beautiful. Confident. Powerful and rightfully me. Validation is a terrible disease. Make sure what you constantly tell yourself is "I love me." And in the midst of that, it doesn't matter who stays or leaves.

# 20 Somethings

I never thought I'd be here, did you? Going through what we go through just to do the things we do. An era where we are more vulnerable than ever. Striving to be more than clever, we are banking on our talents and embarking on business ventures. We are young. We are free. Yet, many of us are still just trying to find our way just to be heard. Just to be seen. We are a marked generation. We have the authenticity of those that thrived in the 90s. Yet some aren't taken seriously because many of us still have the face of a preteen. We are in between. Caught in the middle of fresh trends and what's now considered old school, we are unique. You are youthful and witty, ready to take on the big city, but we are not naïve we can admit within ourselves, which isn't easy.

We are a generation that finds themselves healing more often than not. We recognize that we have a ton that we deal with that others do not. Trying to gain wealth, trying to tend to mental, emotional and physical health and maintaining relationships from family to friends with very little help. It's exhausting. It's border line insane. Yet we wake up each day, and we are prompted to do it all over again. We are still trying to work a day job and still find time to pursue a career. We are in and out of love more times than we can say for ourselves this year. Living through riots, social uproars and racially sensitive climates. We are active, loud and we long to make a difference. We have seen enough and fight the battle no matter how tough.

We are inclined to know more about finances, entertainment, and letting go of our past self. We have acquired a new definition of self-love and disregard what is being fed by the media. Many of us are not where we want to be. We haven't found the right footing that gives our lives the ultimate meaning. Many of us still are single and are looking for the right thing. Many of us have quit love because we are convinced it isn't worth the suffering. And that 20 somethings are supposed to be filled with the good life and the bright lights. But soon, that catches up to us. We are getting older, and the other side of the bed tends to get a little colder.

We open up when the time is right, and we are aware of what we want. We go after it no matter the risk. In love and everywhere else, inspiration lives. I never thought I'd be here, did you? Capturing a daydream behind a computer screen. We should make the most of it. Make the most of a good thing. Staying active and manifesting the God thing. That's what I've learned to do with my 20 something.

# Who Loves Me?

Whether or not you are here, I will always have someone near. I know you wanted to make sure I knew you let go, but ego has a way of sticking around to sharpen the blow. How often will I be controlled by the subconscious things you do? You're not even here, and yet the control you have on me has me scared. Scared that if I don't do all that I can, I can't show you that I couldn't find the same things I found in you in any other man when you left.

How deep down I wished you came back. But isn't that the imposter? Claiming the one that needs the vaccine is also the doctor. We have to admit we both need healing. That where you are, you need to battle your demons. That whether I am there or not, there's always someone listening. Listening to your pain and helping you through your shame. That your pride really is the thing that pushed me away. We were bruised in our own way. And things wouldn't be any easier if you stayed. We both needed to heal. And it takes distance to do so. To be a good person regardless of who's down and who finds the door. It's odd to me that when people throw themselves at a relationship, they neglect themselves all the more. That what matters to them no longer matters anymore. What we need is balance. That we, too, need to find the right footing in what we are leaving and what we are after. Wholeness.

This has to be a new chapter. This, in its own sense, is a rapture. Coming forth into what holds us together and finding we have to be the new master. Of our emotions. Our identity and how often we are open. To those that love us and to those we have yet to hear it spoken. I'm sorry. I had to let you go when you let go of me. It took me some time, but I say out oloud, your mind games can no longer haunt me. I am taking things for what is and taking ahold of what can be. I didn't arrive here on my own, but I found a new song rather in prayer and supplication. I wanted to be free. I had to do what's best for me. Whether you wanted to come back or strengthen your stance to leave. I had to show myself that someone will always love me. Even if that person is me.

# I think I'm Ready

I think I'm ready. I'm ready to put to rest what I find myself in and put on new skin. Laying to bed the old ways I've been living in and pick up some new habits instead. I can no longer try what I used to get me by because it further hides the art of embarking on something new. I think I'm ready. I think I'm ready to learn how to love you. And not in the way that I thought I had to, but in the way that you need me to. It cannot be assumed that the way I want to is how you're used to. And you are quite different. Different from what I'm used to. Quiet and misunderstood, the approach was quite honest, and I can say I never saw it coming.

That a simple encounter would transform into a worthwhile embrace. Grin on your chin and a smile on your face, that's more than nice, but that's not the goal. My desire is to edify your soul. And I didn't mind that this journey would be slow. That you had something over you that you wouldn't let anything easily show. A barrier. A fortress with heightened security. Your heart coated in silence, and your eyes filled with sadness. I saw something different than the others did. And I couldn't put my finger on it, but it was something I always knew. Secrets that your lips would never tell, you wore them on your sleeves so well. Shaping your existence, but with me, you lost all resistance. Something you thought you'd never do. Yet it happened before you even knew. It happened so soon. And with each exchange, our warmth grew. In its own way, we would sway as our differences were allowed in this union that we made.

I think I'm ready. I wanted to take a step back and examine what it would take. A text message from a distance or a moment where you talked, and I just listened. At times in your dismay, I really wanted to do things my way, but I knew that's not what it would take. You needed a safe space. Someone that wouldn't judge you for the weird, quirky decisions you'd make. Unafraid of any of your huge mistakes and allowing grace to heal you after a long day. And I realized that. The heart is fragile, and so is the mind, so I picked it up quickly, that it's important to be kind.

I think I'm ready. Ready to see you as a human being, a man with so much weight on his shoulders that only gets heavier as he gets older. I think I'm ready. To lighten the load and to be your cover. Because when it's all said and done, the day out there may be over, but I know it's important to shield your wounds from any more exposure. I think I'm ready. I think I have what it takes. To finally be present to hold you and see past the cold exterior you built due to what the world has told you. I think I'm ready. I think what's left to ask is, are you ready to receive? I'm ready for you, but are you ready for me?

# There's More In You

As we walk through life, we can forget that there's more in us. The fight along with the bite. The ability to stand up for what's right. There's more in you. That everything happens for a reason, and that response to it is all up to you. Yes, there's more in you. That when challenges come your way, you can stand up and say, "I was built for this". That the adversity itself isn't enough to make you question whether or not you deserve to stay. There's more in you. That praise is buried deep on the inside of you and is aching to shine through.

That the strength you need to endure is one that can only be understood by a few. There's more in you. That even at rock bottom, something unique can happen. Beneath the rubble and the shame, someone is calling you by your real name. That you've got a fight in you despite what life throws at you. "Chosen, Pre-destined, and Conqueror because it was He that built you this way. Wonderfully and fearfully made, you have what it takes to raise the stakes. There's more in you, and you've got what it takes.

# There's More For You

I pray never to be in the same place, doing the same thing next time around. That where I am currently isn't always where I'll be found. That each and every day, there's a goal that needs to be made. A new level of life that needs to be reached. New depths and new room to breathe with a new way of seeing. Whether large or small, these things that we want, we can go for them all! Make no mistake, it all depends on what you say. That your belief is directly attached to whether you'll grow or if you'll stay. It's all on you, believe it or not, despite what others do, you have the final say.

There's more for you. Anything from health to the wealth, they are all attached to one another in some way. Health on a new level and embark on a new journey. That opening up to making new changes can actually extend your life. By incorporating dark berries, dragon fruit and sea moss, you no longer have to suffer energy loss. There's more for you than meets the eye. It's time to expand the horizons of your view. It's time to take a look at what else makes you, you. What else is there? What else is out there for you? The ability to follow your dreams and finally get the degree. Start a business or a nonprofit organization. Write a book, build generational wealth and become debt-free. There's more for you. More than what you're being offered right now. Despite what you've been through or what it looks like, you can start right now. You can start today. Any boundaries you have right now have to come down one by one. Start by saying to yourself,

"I am worth the more. I am worth the more. And I want what God has in store. I want the more. I can't settle in this life anymore with the way things have been. I know what I want and now I am ready to strive for the more. I am ready for the blessings God has in store."

# Hold on

Hold on. You've been through the fire and the rain, and you've experienced such a high level of pain. Hold on. You've gone through so much, and you're heart is now cold to the touch. Hold on. Yes, it's been a while, but you can sing a new song. Hum a new tune. This life isn't over, and there's so much left for you to do. And everything happens for a reason, some that can question our view. But the Lord is always by your side.

He will comfort you. Hold on. For the Bible instructs us Lean not to your own understanding but in all thy ways acknowledge him and he will direct your path. In him, your strength will last. Hold on. You are equipped to do great things. I see it in you. A diamond in the rough, a spectacular view. Hold your head up high, and always remember there's a word specifically for you. Hold on, I say, it's on its way directly to you.

# When you Return

When you return, I am not the same. I am woven in linen that has been through some things. I am no longer stitched in the youth they used to clothe the naïve. I no longer fill my days with mundane games. How sad of you to think me little when while you were gone I grew. I am a soldier now. Fighting battles you thought I didn't know-how. But in knowing that, I hope it makes you proud. I grew up. I'm stronger now. With each blow, my mind has gone through turmoil and depression. All crafted from your distance because you thought it would teach me a lesson.

Affirming my own worth, I was bruised with thinking I had to handle you with aggression. Each day is a battle, and life is the war. And often, I wish to give in because what I do with each moment matters more. How I should receive you when you walk through that door. When you return, I am not the same. I was angry that you left, but at this point, I am just glad you are ok. I take a step back and consider. That how I want to act, would actually push you away. I learned how not to let my past anger leave a horrible stain. I never wanted my hurt to turn into anything that wasn't supposed to stay. When you return, I am not the same. I do things a different way. I talk things out and handle my disputes face to face. I get to the root, forgive and repeat. I also put my foot down and set a boundary or two. I now act accordingly. I make my adjustments and follow suit. My head aligns with my heart, and my soul does the same.

For the frequency to behave is something I want to continue to engage. This level of maturity is sometimes new even for me. This is new territory, but with this mindset, I can finally see. What it means to be free to feel properly when you return. I am not the same. I was just hurt. I didn't know how to express that, but now I want to leave all that I cannot change in the dirt. I am different now, and so are you. So let's find what connects us now, and now let's follow suit.

# Ready

Here I am. Stronger than before and ready for what the world has to offer. No, I haven't always been this way and it's been quite a journey to get here. I had to battle my own rejection and get past unspoken expectations, but it was worth it. Worth it to see bits of the transformation take place. How unfamiliar this land is. I'm still getting used to this. Finally speaking my mind about the fire that's always been inside. The truth is I used to hide.

All of my emotions, never tapped into, and my heart unspoken. I often referred to the review, what was and what I was used to. It took time to snap out of it and be present. To let things go and let things flow as they ought to. I find it better here. Freer in this land I am learning more about. That as I open up, I am around others that truly love me and that support that my opinions matter. This new feeling I have I want the world to know. This wonder, this power. And that we are no longer going to take being crushed by the world, but instead, the world is ours.

# Life

The ups and downs prove to be the best part. Tugging back and forth, pulling on us in every way. Making us greater. Proving there's still fight left in us. Making us far more sensitive. Taking note of what it means to us. Making us open our eyes. Making us show more grace. Making us see how short life really is. Making us behold the beauty that lives. Life has proven to be quite precious. That each experience comes with its own risks. They add to who we are. The things that make us grow and simultaneously the things that make our hearts hard. The battle within that comes out. Life teaches us what that's all about. Life has shown us we need to respect our elderly and hold them, dear. That they are the wisdom that holds our generations on their shoulders. That they paved the way to help to mold us. They are the foundation. Teaching us the true definition of hard work and dedication.

The sweat on their brow and the breaking of their bones were all for us to follow. They did it for us without asking for anything in return. We owe it to them to love them and support them just as they have supported us just like they did for us. Life has been proven to be quite precious. That the very things

# Be the Bridge

It's about that time to be all that we were called to be. In order to properly use our hands and feet. As vessels to give to those in need. Whether it's advice or buying something nice, we have a responsibility to fill the need. Be the bridge. With it, we can walk into a new possibility. A world that knows a warmth that starts from within. A warmth that is always genuine. Be the bridge. Bringing others as we sit down and make time to uncover plans and past traumas. That confident one may need in order to discover when been buried and may need help to recover. Be the bridge. Be the strong friend. Build a support system. We need this more in our community. And all of this starts with the home. Be the bridge, wherever you go. Be the bridge; you'll never be it alone.

# CHAPTER 4
# INSIDE VOICE

It's about time we started to own the impact that we have. Inside voices have been exercised to get the point across without fear of who hears. That a message can be received not just in your own space but can also be invited by others in theirs. Without fear of the distance or resistance, inside voices can be the sound that carries just about anything. It is the level of your voice that recognizes strength and owns the fact that there are things that need to be expressed at a louder frequency. Things about love, friction, pain and even the limitations we place on other people.

This section is such poems that have allowed for strength to reside while still addressing any resistance inside. Whatever that was wished to be said has been said and challenged by what we believe. In the realm of faith, love, confrontations and limitations, this section calls to action forgiveness at a higher degree. That sometimes, it's not about just the world listening, but honing in on what exactly do you need?

Such poems are more objective, more honed in and tend to be a little more straightforward, containing a call to action of checking in with yourself. Don't be afraid to do so, it's all apart of finding your voice.

# A Heavy Heart

Sometimes it hurts to have a heart like mine. Strong, daring yet lying on a plate outside of my chest, I give my love away. But isn't that what we are supposed to do? Bit by bit, piece after piece, we offer peace by what we grow inside. Aren't we to be patient? And aren't we to be kind. What's mine is yours, and what's yours is mine, so why do I feel misused and so far behind? Nice guys finishing last, and nice girls never crossing the finish line. Over time and overlooked it seems to me I was learning from the wrong book. So I changed the narrative. I decorated my eyelids with glitter and covered my face. With marble, they marveled and finally fixed their gaze on me.

I was finally seen. Engaging in conversations that were beyond me saying things I didn't mean. From being safe to unclean, but isn't that part of doing things? Loosening up and being free? Otherwise, what's really happening? What they refuse to tell you is ambitions misplaced, will surely slap you in the face. Challenging everything you thought you knew. That putting on new skin and acting brand new would actually be a result of the world playing you. But you are not to blame. Insecurities and comparisons were the fuel to that flame. Pop culture, cancel culture and sometimes instant fame. Subconsciously we dodge all responsibility and constantly looking to point the finger. To place blame. Thinking we had to change who we are or what we have to be fully put up on the game. At the end of it all, it is not worth it. Our souls are not a game, and trends constantly change. But we need to keep our eye on what stays the same. Love. Yes, it hurts, and yes there's pain, but aside from all, there's truly more to gain. Placing your attention on your internal care again.

Taking your time to take the proper context from the proper book. Reminding yourself that Yes, love is patient, and love is kind. It does not boast, nor does it brag. It is not redundant, and it does not drag. There are not requirements to get any of it, just receive. Sitting on a plate outside of your chest available to be experienced in its highest measure. Know that your soul is the greatest treasure and they love you freely give is also available for you too.

# So What's Up?

If you're talking about talking instead of actually talking, there's no point in talking. If we're actually going to be talking, then I guess you should start talking.

Do me a favor and start at the beginning. Start by placing your hand on your chest and take a deep breath. Be honest. Take note of how your body stands before me. Are you nervous? Are you at ease? In my presence, do you feel anything other than peace? Work with me. Let's arrive there together, introducing ease. I never meant to harm you. I still had some trauma I was working through. I said things and did things I never tried to. And I'll admit that.

I'm ok admitting I wasn't where I wanted to be. I'm better now. I can face myself in the face and right my wrongs, but only if you let me. Forgiveness is a part of this new journey. Working through the kinks and finding what works because I never meant to make lightly of your trust. Let's talk. Let's finally get it out, find out what the disconnect is all about. Do you feel unworthy? Unready of the good woman that stands before you? Do you feel like you're not ready? That you have to endure all that life has to offer before you take a wife? Let me know!

So I'm not guessing my whole life. If you dance around the idea for much longer, I'll get sick of the music and play a new song. A new tune will do until you come with the truth. And I never meant to disrespect you, but if I don't communicate like this, you may never get my view. That all this time I really cared for you. And I'm sorry for anything my attitude may have put you through. I wish we could start at the beginning and that we could get to the root. But I guess I'll have to leave it open for when you finally respond. That's if you're ready to talk, but that's honestly up to you.

# Limitations

Limitations are internal creations. What I've built up in my mind to box you in, it's amazing how long I've managed to keep you there. I thought that I was doing myself a favor. I placed warning signs in the form of labels, telling myself fables, you would never know I told. Caution tape across my heart, traffic cones redirecting traffic so I wouldn't have any more distractions at the scene of the crime. Limitations. Boxing you in by belief that things would go down the same as last time, you never changed. That rage is the norm; in this book, there is no other page. My experiences have saved me time. I don't have to see another side.

I know what I need to know. There's nothing else left. Yet, what I've done to you, who's to say you haven't done also? That my shut down when problem arises, you take my disposition with no surprises. That my own depression comes after a spell of unrequited aggression, these mood swings could never be your favorite past time yet they happen all the time. And in your mind, you've shackled me, a victim of a selfish crime. Limitations, we create in our mind, I'm sorry. I wanted to protect myself, but instead, it did the opposite. Creating boxes leaving things up for interpretation instead of hashing things out. Limiting beliefs that whatever box I put you in, you wouldn't want out.

I'm sorry. I assumed the worse instead of allowing you to plead your case with your own mouth. Limitations. That you'd never change no matter how much you really wanted to. No matter how much you worked too. I'm sorry. That my manifestations worked against you. That I am more powerful than I mean to be. That's what's true, is your internal healing means so much to me. I'm sorry. That the limitations I placed on you would question the journey of growth you have to go through. I'm sorry. And I hope you would have the strength to forgive me just as I had the strength to believe the reality you serve me is true.

# Needs No Convincing

Your job is not to convince anyone of anything. Your job in life is to just be. All that you are and evolve into who you can be. No need to convince someone of the goodness they know you to possess. It shows up on your face. Finds its way in your actions during your normal day to day. A heart of gold that cannot be broken. A warmth that cannot be shaken. I know you to be so open, but it isn't your job to convince the broken. Your job in life is not to try to be anything other than the goodness you possess. I know you to be your best. And yes, life has a way of throwing you a test. But that's the time to say it with your chest. To rise to the occasion, no contest. If you are understanding, be that. If you are strong-willed, be that. If you are cool, calm and collected, there's room for that too. There's nothing you have to convince the world of, nothing to hide, nothing to prove. All the best lies inside and longs to shine through.

# Distance

In this new day and age, we've learned to keep our distance. That the new love we show in our persistence. For human connection, we now have to make recollections on what kept us together in the past. That the times we are in now, those times no longer last. Things are different now. We have to wear masks now. We often hide our faces because of a disease that means "crown".

Our royalty is defined by who can obey. New laws and new regulations changing every day. We now have to love one another from 6 feet away to avoid sending each other 6 feet under. Because at this distance, our love is considered safe. Our love is undisputed and unrequited, but at least it helps reduces cases. This distance has taught me to behave. That my love for you must now be intentional, and I have to watch where I go. That whatever I pick up may have an effect on you in some way.

This is something I know. That human warmth is something I crave. There is a ministry in being held with a hug from a friend. Or a loved one that has often been so far away. I've learned that I must love you from afar to keep you safe. Even if this is the norm, for now, I have the opportunity to be more intentional. I must remember the warmth of my love can still reach you somehow. Although I see this as a chance to slow down, I can be present with each interaction. That I can lean in more to listen. And I can watch my boundaries and pay more close attention. This is a new day and age, and the norm now is to keep our distance. That we must show love as often as we can. In this, we must be persistent.

# You Didn't Break Me

You didn't break me because you didn't make me. I could never possess what you never gave me.

How at first glance, it was by chance that it ended this way. When now, we reminisce on how we used to speak day to day.

How a "have a good night" and a "good morning" texts weren't too far away.

Now it's all a distant memory. That by chance you now have something that belongs to me,
My sanity.

My prized possessions happened to be barely breathing normal air because I'm used to the flames. Heat through my fangs, you've pissed me off, you've made me angry, you've made me sad, you've made me cry, but you weren't supposed to…

Because how dare you, you shouldn't be able to break me.
Cus' clearly you didn't make me. So how could I give

you credit for what you never gave me?
My sanity.
My clarity.

My bold acquisition, inquisitive tongue, breathing hellfire, boarding a streetcar named desire. You obviously felt threatened by my necessity for clarity. I'd be mad too if I challenged me the way I challenged you. How it's too cute. How it gets, you used to opening up and telling the truth. Pulling back layers of tales with unrequited love and tearing down your walls with big brown eyes while batting large lashes, your defenses are down. You've lost your strength now. Samson at wits end because I'm stronger now than when I began.

Why?
Because I got a hold of what's precious to me.

My sanity.
I had to remember truly that you didn't break me
Because you.... you never made me.

And I will never give you credit for what you never gave me.

# All Along

I guess it's true. You kiss a couple of toads before you get to the truth. Not about him, but about you.

Who you are, what you possess and who you've been from the start. That you just can't help it. That sometimes your soul intertwines with your heart.

An excusable mess but a wonderful work of art. Both repelling and compelling. See, you are the rose, and your goals and aspirations are the thorns.

Protecting you from those not destined to hold you. You're growing in their very presence, while your very essence is destined to bud beautifully.

One day, one may be intimidated by that. See, he saw you as a challenge or a big relief. You got him with your big brown eyes, sweet smile and crisp white teeth.

After a few meetings, a couple of greetings, messages and confessions, you're hoping for progression. Only to meet regression in the sign of rejection.

But look at how God does it, it was only the hand of his protection. See, your rose wasn't meant to be picked yet.

You're still growing. You're still producing fruit. Blossoming and coming into your true molding. Something worth firmly holding regardless of how large, sharp, or intense your thorns can become.
Dare to do.
Dare to be.

Regardless of who stays and regardless of who leaves. Their distance from you had nothing to do with you. Let them be. Their vacancy is only making room for the right things to come, and with the proper eyes, who can see. So if they want to, let them leave. Then take your time. Cry, this was a worthy death to grieve. Cus' when you kissed that frog, you were hoping for a prince.

Truth is, it didn't happen because you were meant for a King. If you don't get anything else, just know that every thought, every request, the Lord hears them all. With time, it'll all come to pass. They'll recognize sooner or later, all along, they were in the presence of a Queen.

# The Unseen

We are often fooled by what we don't see. As the sun sets and the moon rises, I'm prompted to challenge this world's unbelief. That the wonders of this world are tangible mysteries. Just like the raw potential, it lives on the inside of me. Only hoping and wishing to find a true identity. I guess that's why there's true power in belief. I wonder what is your superpower? What would you wish for if it arrived today? To fly? Move things with your mind? How about going back in time. Right wrongs and stop crime? To teleport and finally take that trip you were planning up north. It's crazy. How we can dream of these things now. But what we neglect to realize is we had this imagination all along. Even as young babies.

The gift of Manifest and that we can do this on a daily. I urge you, challenge the world's definition of "maybe". Maybe I can fly, or maybe I will get my dream job or marry my dream guy. Challenge the world's definition of maybe. Maybe I'll succeed, or maybe I'll try. Step out of yourself and discover your why. And let faith arise. Because we will always be fooled by what we don't see. But no matter what, there's greatness on the inside of you and me.

# Faith Can Be Tricky

Faith… that can be really tricky. I often wondered if it were just me. If people would think I was crazy. Saying things that contradicted what I see. Speaking things that haven't yet transpired, but I can help it. I can't help my deep down desire. Seeing my family free. Healing on a new degree. Generational wealth enters my bloodline but to believe something bigger than me sometimes feels like a crime. That the energy of the air is a current, I must follow. Anything other than would result in punishment.

That I would be reprimanded for wanting more and requiring more from my environment. Breaking through is all I know, yet I am afraid at my own might. My will to fight. By any means necessary, even if that means defeating my own mind, my biggest adversary. I'm afraid I'd win because I am wonderfully and fearfully made. Because id being loosed from your chains wakes up the neighborhood and gives them something to say. I can't help but muster up the courage to break free. But this freedom isn't just for me. I want it for everyone. So come join me. And I know faith can be really tricky. We are getting used to trusting what we don't see. But we have yet is to marvel at finally being free.

It doesn't take much. Finding the warmth in a worthy embrace. It doesn't take much. Finally, taking the chance to put down pride and let love reside. It doesn't take much. To right my wrong and admit that you're right. I am as mighty a being as you say. I am strong, and I am as kind-hearted as they say. The gem in my chest is three sizes too big and continues to grow. Spreading and stretching across valleys and horizons, impacting everyone it touches. And I know it doesn't take much.

In order to change a life and touch another soul. A passing glance or a soft touch. I thought I knew the impact you had on me. With that same impact, I, too, have on you. I never knew the reality of who I really am until now. There's a deep desire within me to show wear the crown. Show the royalty we were born in and touching the world, starting by showing self-love from within. Self-care so that one day we can dare to be our true selves. Mighty beyond measure. Not afraid of our internal treasure. It doesn't take much. A sincere touch and the ability to trust.

# Vision

What do you see? Write it down, make the vision plain. Get it all out. Jot it down. Get specific, all the way down to the air that you breathe. What do you see? That what you see is the measure of what you believe. Then it begs the question, what do you believe? Do you believe that you can achieve anything? That in this lifetime you can accomplish your dreams? What do you see? All the way down to the physical things. What do you want? A large house? A faithful spouse? A backyard with a view? How about the job of your dreams. The one that lets you take a long vacation or two.

Do you know yourself to be a visionary? Creating constantly? That what you dream isn't only reserved for your sleep. That what you come up with is a beautiful dream that doesn't need to be met with disbelief. Vision gives you aim. It gives you something to look forward to. Something to behold. And sometimes, these visions can be scary. They often are bigger than us and can weigh on us heavily. But there's hope in seeing them come to life one day. By breaking it down. Bit by bit and realizing what can be done today. That each piece in important to the whole picture, and it takes time for it all to come in place. And it can. Just give it time. Just make sure you write it down.

# The Cost

Worthy of exchange in order to embrace change, what we seek will give our future range. In recent time I've found that life has a lot of moments. Moments strung together in time laced together by things that matter. A warm embrace bringing a smile across your face, we danced the night away. Times were simpler. Most moments started at dinner. Accompanied by candlelight, a simple fire. Sparking my interest deepened my desire not to stay there but inspire. And it weighs on me.

In my private time, inspiration comes to my mind. Calling me and stretching on the inside. An early birth that was soon to arise. It dawned on me that I have seed. And it is growing on the inside of me. I've tried to make reason with it. And I've tried to confess it to those around me. That the more and more I go over it, it changes. It morphs into a new creation, and I lose sight of the initial seed. The cost. Of being a worthy vessel, sometimes you lose sleep.

Sometimes I've seen things, and when I try to others, they struggle to see. Often times have no idea what you mean. Often times I lose sleep. Excitement fills my body, and I'm energized beyond definition. And all of this is new to me. That what A lot of things won and a lot of things lost. Things in this life are gonna' cost. It might be small, it might be large, but it will be required to make it to your next.

# What Is It?

Why do we try to convince the people that hurt us, they had no right to hurt us? They hurt us because they did not know the true versions of who we really are. Who's to say that if they truly knew us, they wouldn't have still hurt us the way they did and at the capacity in which they did so, if not more? If not less? Regardless. Why do we haggle with the devil? Why do we go back and forth with the ones that don't deserve us? And reason with them they don't? It's madness. Madness, I tell you. What is it? It is them we are trying to convince that we are worthy? Or are we trying to convince ourselves as we speak out loud? Why can't we walk away? Why do we entertain the madness? It's madness with very little to gain. All of this, designed to run a rat's race. I'm telling you it isn't worth it. Not anymore. We can finally let them go. We can, and we will.

# Focus

It's time we maintained a focus on what mattered. That these things that entertained us in the past have no right to do so anymore. Such toxic games we play knowing someone wants us, but we don't want them in return. Not being honest with ourselves when the true answer to a question or request is "No". Neglecting those that are in our lives that truly need our help. How can we get our focus back on what matters? By first identifying what does. Paying attention and noticing what's going on in our bodies and in our world. What brings happiness, and what brings ease. What causes growth curing a notable disease. What is causing us to grow, and what is leaving us empty.

It takes some time and honest evaluation. That such things we have more control over than we gave ourselves credit. But it's time to pivot and make an adjustment. It's time to focus on what truly matters. Those that are in our lives to stay. Those relationships that need maintenance. Those projects that need to be released or even our mental and physical health. Our relationships and being comfortable enough to call on them for help. Noticing a sudden shift and reasoning with the seasons on what's next. Being prepared to leap when God says go. Having our eyes on the things that helped us grow. Having a heart of gratitude no matter where we go. These are the things that matter. These are the things I hope you know.

# Intentionality

When you make a decision about something, how strong is it? How about a promise? How strong are the roots to keep it? That which you speak are reflective in whether or not you really mean it. Intention is key. Intention is necessary. It gives reason to the roots that run deep. The why? What it truly means inside. I can tell you that I'd never want to hurt you again, but I have to identify my why so it never happens again. Is it the tears? Is it the pain? Or maybe desire to see you smile again.

My resolve gives me direction from here on out. This resolve has to be unwavering that nothing shakes it. That no circumstance or no challenge breaks it. What an anchor is to a boat, so are my intentions, and they must be felt and shown. In order to do so the right way, I just need to figure out what I want to see at the end in the beginning. A goal worth winning, a visionary in the beginning. This not only brings clarity to the situation but also grants the other person peace of mind. Intentionality gives your decisions depth and width, giving you something meaningful to work with. So the next time you make a decision, ask yourself, how strong is it? How about a promise? How strong are the roots, and can you keep them?

# Revelation

Between the lost and found, there is only but a thin difference. And that is a revelation. Coming into the realization that reality is more than meets the eye. It is incomplete. There are experiences that fill in the gap of our understanding and make way for what we truly mean. And there are times where things happen, and we have to catch up as to why they did. The bridge of our understanding. Revelation. That all things don't go wasted and all turn out for the good of those it happens to.

That loss, that break up, those people leaving your life, all meant to happen to reveal the remedy of such strife. That your noble character is not dependent on who stays and who leaves. That the pain you felt, when placed in the hands of those who care, can really prove to be a safe place for you. And when people leave, it makes room for the right ones to appear. Or even shed light on the ones who are left. How often we miss so much when we only have tunnel vision. Make room for revelation. Make room for understanding. Take time to figure out why things happened and what that experience brought out of you. I know many of them are great things but are they great to you?

# What To Do

What do you do when nothing seems to be working? That everything you've done now has left you so open. Open to so many emotions. That when they stand on their own, they don't quite make sense. Such are mixed emotions. I've always wondered what to do with the moment. That standing alone doesn't do what I thought it was supposed to. Or even burying it in business all of a sudden. I always wanted to more for this moment. I wanted the remedy of being so broken. It's hard. Not knowing what to do when nothing seems to be working. Instead, I'm left with observing my rearview. That the past has something that my future not yet has. Filled with moments where I was always cutting it close. Rent due, bills due and not working enough hours too. Yet I remembered how much God came through.

How he provided and how he sat with me when I wasn't sure of what I would do. How grace came and comforted my loved ones when I was unable. All of the good things. All without fault, he held us up when we weren't able. When nothing seems to be working, you get a reminder of what always has and what always will. That this moment is no different. That this moment holds no question and all the lesson. Have a spirit of gratitude no matter what gets you stressing.

# CHAPTER 5
# PROJECTION

Projection happens when you are sure of your message. A fire is ignited from within, and you are convicted in what you believe. That the message you wish to express is no longer foreign to you. It is also a call to who we really are and a necessity to come forth. In these poems, such situations are explored in a way to call notice to change. How to conduct yourself around constant change, let go, and take advantage of such a chance to be proud of yourself. That any message in repetition can be a positive one and can be a reflection on yourself. It's time to project what truly matters.

This section was constructed to shed light on our actions and what we now must be able to do with our lives and to help put things in their proper perspectives. Don't be afraid to ask yourself the hard questions. Don't be afraid of what lessons await for you.

# Perspective

Please listen. There are things you pursue and things that pursue you. Know the difference. Things you attract, and things because of you are in existence, please hear me. Make the vision clear. Let it have its arrival because its lives will be changed and chains will break, it's very vital. For the generational narrative to be shifted into a new point of view. Study. Listen and listen clearly. This view I'm giving you will change the world. Be a willing vessel. Things are supposed to come to you in order to come through you.

# Outside of Ourselves

We have the tendency to see our own circumstances come to the edge of our world. That an avalanche of disbelief can overtake us, overshadowing our perspectives. That our issues are more than what they are. Yes, they are valid. And yes, they matter. But if we get so worked up on what is happening on the inside of us, we miss out on our outside world. The issues of poverty and homelessness are not just an external disease.

Poverty is staying in debt with no room to breathe. Not adding to the lives of others and solely focusing on material things. Taking away from others and leaving them with no hope only curates an endless cycle of suffering. Homelessness is finding refuge outside of yourself. Not feeling safe within because of the debt waiting to be paid to society. Holding up your end of the deal to be a puppet on a string adding to the bodies in the grave because you got to live a happy life but not a long one. Homelessness is forgetting who you are on earth and rejecting your projection of heaven. Laying the power at the doorstep of humility because it makes other people safer where they are.

Making them feel better, they don't have to go so far because this life has proven to be so hard. But you? you've got to break barriers. You've got to act on the truth. Battle homelessness and poverty don't accept a truce. Combat it with what needs to be used. Your words. Speaking life over yourself by any means necessary. Planting seeds of green and start by being encouraging. Uplift your brothers and your sisters. We are all we got. Your actions. Give of your resources, time and energy. Show people, they are worth it. Let love be long-suffering. Be patient for what we deal with on a daily isn't an easy thing. Your belief. In mankind to be all that we can be as beautiful human beings. That underneath all the mess, we are royalty and destined to be thriving kings and queens.

God wants this for everybody. So allow him to do great work in you. I promise it's a great thing.

# The Power of Repetition

Repetition is powerful. Laying down the law in a way that drives the message home. "Take out the trash", "do the dishes," and "wash your face." All tasks, with time, we wish our parents would cease to say. Until it's replayed in our minds on an odd day. What else did they once say? "I'll be there for you always", "don't worry, I've got you." And the disciplinary "eat all the food off your tray……look at me all you want to but unless you finish it. You can't go out and play". A past time. And it's moments like these we'd wish they'd go away.

That what they had to say would make sense in time. There's a lesson in repetition. That with each message, there was something to learn. That there was a difference in getting things owed to you and others you earned. It amazes me. That sometimes, we forget what a true lesson does. And that's to bring the best out of you. That patience really is a virtue. Patience does everything but hurt you. Growing roots digging deep in the discipline. Following instruction, paying attention and challenging mental retention. Stretching your capacity and prompting tenacity, it's amazing what our parents can tell us that come to meet us when we need it most.

Repetition, repetition, you have a duality that I must respect. You can love and haunt. That what was said to me I long to forget. Anything that entered into my mind a youth designed to break me down, has a tendency to bring a current frown. I fight the urge to drown. Right where I am, I battle the tool of repetition with my own again. Repeating what I know to be true and how perseverance has brought me where I am. I am loved. I am worthy. I am strong. That as time passed, I right was previously wronged. I know I am in this place for a reason. I love that I am here for this season. Repetition thank you for your ways. Thank you for brightening my days and capturing the sun rays. Thank you. I appreciate you always.

# Do That

That which makes you happy, do that.
That which makes your heart race, do that.
That which may make you afraid but can promise to be a great escape, do that.
That which challenges your character and deepens your faith, do that.
That which grants you breathing space and can make this life a worthwhile race, do that.

Have that hard conversation that can no longer wait, do that. Put down your pride and repair what can be fixed today, do that.

As you can see, time is of the essence, and some things can no longer be taken as lightly.

If you don't do anything else, can you do that?

# Be The Inspiration

What about the children? A small voice heard in the distance, hoping you'll listen. They need you. Your warmth, your guidance, your consideration peeking. What about the children? They need help too? Their wish to use their voices just the way you do. Would you mind? Helping those that need it? Reaching out their hand as they get ready to receive it. I'm not sure you quite understand or can quite see it. That children are quite impressionable, and they copy something when they see it. The way you address them with love and with care. They will grow up to do the same all because you were simply there. It's about being an example. Being available to love.

This can start with an encouraging word, a worthwhile embrace or a hug. They see you as their inspiration because of how you live your life. With every goal you set, you run a worthy stride. With a large smile and glitter in their eyes, you've done something remarkable. You planted a seed they buried deep inside. They see how you handle life, when you meet your goals and when you don't have any strength left. How you spend your time and what you feed your soul. They see it all. And they consider it all gold. You are an amazing human being. I hope you know. Take advantage of the time it takes to show. The audacity of this time we have to let our young ones know. That you can do and be just about anything. Be the light they need to be. Be their motivation. Be the inspiration.

# Let's Not Fight It

There is a sunset for every sunrise. That with deep sighs, there's deep cries hoping others who are strong would pull us up. That especially in those times, true glory and divinity still reside. I find beauty in beginnings, but I also find the grace when they also find their ending. Bonds and ties can't be broken unless we give in to their proper season. Something I wish I didn't have to accept unless it was for the right reason. But I'm learning to let things be. That what works really does work is really what's best for me. When friends move on or loved ones leave, I used to feel pain. So deep and endured a lot of suffering, but I learned that what lied within me was something great. My heart. The ability to love regardless of what happened.

That I had the choice and chance to love from a distance safe for the both of us. That the relationship can have its proper place. This, to me, is the best type of grace. That my love doesn't have to be forced. That regardless of distance, it can still have the greatest force. The hardest part is forgiving yourself for what residue still resides between you and me.

What I wanted to say and what I actually got the chance to express. Wanting the chance to get it all off my chest. The truth is, I still can; although you may not be in the audience, my announcement still stands, and I can go about this the right way. That I can let go and let the sunset on its right time. After all, I can look back and enjoy myself when I did have a sunrise.

# Keep On Going

We need you. What you have and all that you are, make up a worthy leader. A teacher. Ready to give the greatest life lesson. We've all watched from an outside view, what's your secret? Do you make a schedule for every day and repeat it? Make a promise to yourself and do your best to keep it? We all want to know! How do you get to the place of constant results?

That whatever you set your mind to, favor follows. We no longer want to continue down a path that leaves us hollow. We'll admit we had a tendency to create toxic trends and wallow. And let pride get in the way, but this time, we'll swallow. All the things that are standing in our way, and take heed of the constructive things you have to say.

We are all ears! And I assure you we can't wait. And you took the time to pull up a chair and leaned in so we can listen close:
 "Keep On Going. Yes, keep on moving forward. For the race isn't given to the swift nor the strong, but to the ones that endure to the end. And this is key.

Making sure when the things in life are thrown at you, you can endure high levels of pain and unjust suffering. To make sure what it is you, is really what you say is there. Keep on Going. Persistence is the sauce. And without it, your goals and intentions will be lost. The muscles to pull your weight will be clear in the action that you take. Holding everything in place, for the Lord's sake. He will see you through, despite some of the things you will go through, but this is what truly keeps me. My goal was never the things I acquire, but instead the will and desire to inspire. Every day I live for this moment to stand before you. Sharing how I won the moment. Keep on Going. Just keep on Going."

# They Can't Handle It

I just came over to say hello. Nothing more, nothing less. I never wanted to take anything from you, just get that off my chest. I only wanted to give because that's all my heart knows how to do. I am a good person, despite the hardships I go through. The funny thing is, in little time, you picked up on that too. I wanted to learn how to love you better and take time out to learn your love language too. How to fill your cup and speak life into you on a daily. But I can tell that where you are today, that's too much, and you're simply not ready.

Sometimes we have the purest intentions, and sometimes we encounter those that aren't ready. Ready to receive the love we are so ready to give and the love we have. Those who reject it make us second guess the heart that we have. That we are too soft or have to grow cold bones, so we don't get taken advantage of. The truth is, we do ourselves a disservice if we let this trend continue. Never let someone make you feel like you aren't worth it because your love was too strong for them. You did what you knew how and you must forgive yourself for what did not work or what went wrong. It was out of your control. It's not your fault. Forgive them, forgive yourself and do your best to move on. Who you are is who your future spouse needs. And if they don't have the eyes to behold who you are, chances are they weren't meant to see. Sometimes what happens is they know you are husband or wife material, and they let you free. And it's frustrating! It's not fair to pick up your own heart every time someone else makes it bleed. I can assure you, there is one thing they may never tell you. You made a lasting impression on their heart, and they will treat the world differently because of you. That your encounter alone made them a better man or woman, and their pride won't let that show.

Sometimes these encounters happen just so that people's eyes are open and to allow us to see the gem on the inside of you. That we are a gift that should never be mishandled or misused. That since we have this gift, it is time to set healthy boundaries and recognize its power. It shouldn't go to just anybody, and we are allowed to qualify our space. That we have a stay of who we want around and who we want to stay. We have the right to observe who can handle our love and who cant.

# Don't Forget to Live

Don't forget to live! Don't forget to take it all in and engage your senses. Don't forget to live. That with each day, you have something precious to give. A warm smile, a hug and even some advice you could enlighten someone else with. Don't get so wrapped up in what was and in what could not be changed. Just as equally, don't get too stressed out about what else has yet to be lived. Both the future and the past have their place, and let's be active and leave it where it is. And live. Go for a walk in your favorite neighborhood.

Circle the block once or twice. Notice how our environment doesn't fight itself. It works together with each other's help. This flow, this effortlessness. Is something we hope to touch others with. Don't forget to live. Just as equally, take a risk! Do something you never have before and enjoy every minute of it. Find a new hobby like paint and sip. Or try something extreme by jumping out of a plane. Whatever you do, don't forget to live. Don't forget to be fully present and allow creativity to flow. New ideas will sweep your world and introduce a new glow. You deserve all that life has to offer, especially now. Don't forget to live. Don't forget to live.

# Stay Moving

Look forward. Stop looking back at what was in regretting what went wrong. Let go. Move on, not for them but for you. You deserve to have an uninterrupted view of the promise ahead of you. That your relationship with time should be a good one. The past, filled with good times and lifelong lessons. Please hear me. Your past cannot be changed, but it changes who you are each time you look back that far.

What went down, what went wrong. Played over and over again like a bad love song, strongholds are formed, and you exercise your inability to let go of what hurt you. Running around in circles, playing over and over like a broken record. Bad dates and times you cheated on your diet with a piece of birthday cake. Small failures with big definitions giving you the wrong rendition and outlook on life. Let go. Move on. Not for them but for you.

That what you went through isn't just for you. Do me this one favor. If you stay in the past, learn from it and tell a story to another young person a lesson we know will last. Tell them who you became and what new experiences you are taking in your now. That's why your present is so important. It is the gift of time. With each moment, second, hour, minute, there's a worthy surprise in it. Wrapped in exchange meant to bring out a charm in you not to disregard what you've been through. A chance to engage and listen, go all in. Because people really do care if the whole time you've been listening. Don't give up.

For in the present, you can be ready for whatever comes your way. Quick on your toes and ready for anything, being present allows you to take your environment in. Smelling the roses. That soft moment of silence that offers you blissful peace. It's marvelous here. So enjoy each time that you get here. Because the future can't take care of itself. Things that have yet to be grasped and experienced. Let them linger in the distance, for now. Gauge when you are ready for it, truthfully. What you can handle today and what you can transition into smoothly. It's not too unruly. It's like a slow-mo movie. The future is what you make of it as long as you keep moving. Look forward.

Stop looking back and regretting what went wrong. I promise you the future is bright. Start focusing on what went right. Be empowered by your ability to create something new. That it really does work on the inside of you. Start looking at time as a safe place. To get things done and to add on to your experiences too. I assure you. As you look forward, you become empowered, and this is the last day you are taunted like you are a coward. You have the freedom to be inspired. This is the time to dream. It's time to dream with your eyes open. That the reality you seek will come to pass once spoken. Just make sure when you see it that you receive it. Recognize it and believe it. Be sure to open up your eyes to see it.

# Gratitude

I'm thankful! For all the things that took place and all the things that didn't! For all the twists and turns that took place, for without them, I'd be so different. I wouldn't have this calm disposition. I'd be too tough, and I'd be so hard-headed with no desire to listen. My life would be so different. I wouldn't have been able to make sense of why I was shielded from the world at such a young age. And why I couldn't have social media accounts like the other girls my age. I would have been rushed to grow up and misbehave. Instead, my father kept me in sports, I knew exactly how to stay busy.

I balanced academic clubs, sports and involvement in school. I rarely dated, and I kept my cool. I often compared myself to those that did what I wanted to do. I was different, and I always knew. But looking back, I'm thankful for it! Because in those boundaries, I grew! I learned through others on what to do and what not to do. How I learned from others' pain by sitting in it with them. An empathetic friend to the pain. How I developed an outside view to hold them up and see them through. I was thankful! To be with them when they needed me most. And as time went by, I would learn I could lean on them too.

I'm thankful! For all the things that took place and all the things that didn't! For all the twists and turns that took place, without them, I'd be so different. That had I not gone to college, I wouldn't know how to handle commitment. Commitment to my word and to adjust to the outside world. I was no longer a kid living under my parent's roof, yet I would always be their baby girl. I had to take more accountability for my mistakes. That they were things that I had to make unless I wouldn't learn anything at all. Failures and shortcomings, life testing me to see if I'd fall. If I'd bend or if I'd crawl. I had to be tough. I chose to endure it all. I faced my fears, and I even cried once or twice through them all. I had many sleepless nights and brain farts where I wasn't fully aware of what was happening. I worked relentlessly because that's what I always knew how to do. I even began diving into what I liked, went to a poetry event or two. Had I not gone through any of this, I wouldn't have unlocked a dormant gift. I would never have known the seed that needed to be watered.

I'm thankful! For all the things that took place and all the things that didn't! For all the twists and turns that took place, without them, I'd be so different. I wouldn't know that I often get homesick and that as my parents get older, I too must get bolder. That I have no time to waste, but I mustn't get anxious, always looking over my shoulder. My parents taught me to be a go-getter and always be kind. You never know who you'll meet or who you're leaving behind. It tough! Having to take care of business, isolate yourself, work long, long hours to make ends meet. That's the price you pay when you have a journey laid out for you not destined for the weak. I am stronger than I know. And there's still so much left inside to grow. I'm thankful for the bumps and bruises and the chance to give it all I got. I know my time is now, to give it my best shot.

# Kindness

Be kind always. For people who are nearest to us are fighting hardships we often know nothing about. Battles to where we would see ourselves out. Be kind always, for in it is the remedy we all need that often comes in the smallest seed. A small gesture is all one needs. Someone buying your groceries or a small cup of coffee. A compliment on their outfit or a kind word or two. A word of encouragement in passing, not trying to stay too long or take up their time. We never know what someone needs or how long that need was there.

A text or a call to make someone's day, fulfilling a need their way. Specific to another, not imposing what you want but taking the time to ask them what fills their cup. "Do you need a hug? Do you need a friend" Ask them what they need so you can be there as a better friend. Be kind always. You never know what someone is going through. Some days may be off days, and you're short on words to say. It has nothing to do with the other person; you just may not want to communicate. And it's not your fault; you only long for someone to understand.

This is where a kind gesture can go a long way. Communicate that you haven't given up on them and that you can love them from a distance, let them have this day. Be kind always. You never know what someone is going through. What losses they endured or what disrespectful encounters happened before encountering you.

Take a deep breath, and ask them if they are ok. Invite them to talk about it, don't make them open up right away. Just take your time and wait. Don't be afraid of the emotions they express at the moment, and don't shy away. Let them know you love them even in the silence you stay. In due time they will open up, even if it isn't right away. Some process things internally; they just do things a different way. No matter what the reasons are and what they go through. Be kind always.

# What My Self Never Knew

I never got that chance to sit down with myself and tell her how proud I am of her. That she was dealt difficult cards yet did her best regardless. She's seen long hours inside the four corners of her apartment for long hours on end with nowhere to go. Homeschooling kept the mental and emotional distance between her and other kids. The hardship of letting others in as she got accustomed to the big world that awaited her outdoors. I never noticed how afraid she was.

To be lost in an abyss and being drowned out by the noise of other kids. She was the quietest one. How it shaped her. How it molded her. And how sometimes it shut her up from speaking up when wrong was done to her. How she endured. How she found her voice in the passion of not being forgotten. With each inch of the time she found her strength in two words a day no three. With time she found the world deserving of what she had to offer. Before long, she got comfortable raising her hand. She asked questions. She became the loudest daughter. She grew a love for the men in her life, starting with her father and farther she'd go to the outside world to see that there more in this life for this little girl.

At the time, I didn't know how to talk to you. I just watched from a birds-eye view. How we struggled below. But you never let that stop you; you never ceased to glow. I'm happy for you. I know sometimes you grow tired, but you never get weary of well-doing. No matter the circumstance or what the devil may be brewing. I am certain that you go to the right people when you yourself have no idea what you should be doing. You seek council now. You do your best to make mama proud. I'm excited now. You are a happy child. Deep down, you just want to make others smile. And I know I never with you and talked to you as a child. But I'm here now. And I know the importance of conversing with your inner self. Take time to do that today.

Look in the mirror and tell yourself, "you make me proud. We've come a long way and ain't no stopping us now. We were never a peasant, but it's time we took the crown. I'm happy for you. You shine now brighter than you have been. You've gone through a lot, endured some suffering. And I'll let you know now, you can relax. Soon we can retire with a ring."

# How To Forgive You.

Just keep going. Find your strength again. There's no problem in looking deep within. I promise it'll help you with all your stress. Take a deep breath; it'll help. I've been where you are, alone and in need. I thought I was a different breed. Some rules just weren't for me. I was a good girl. I toed the time even in my private time. But sometimes, I wanted to do my own thing go my own way. That if I got a little rebellious, it would keep the feeling alive.

That I could hide little secrets that have strengthened my pride. Not knowing anything real was growing, and I fooled even myself. By dwelling in my flesh instead of my spirit. There were things I ran away from, knowing I had to clear it. I have to keep going. I have to find my strength again. That I have to take on the task of looking deep within. That I'm ready to put behind me all the stressing. That golden day. When the skyline of my life is no longer gray. And can look forward to springtime before May. It's now.

I can have this healing now. So you can you. I'll show you how. Make a list of all the things you resist.

Having that conversation or things you regret. And make another. Of all the things you've locked away that now you wish to uncover. And as you approach them, declare these words.

"You had your place in the past but no longer have control over me. I am now making the conscious decision to make amends with the things I can't change and be free. That any hold you had on me, be relinquished now and let go of me. I am now planting a new seed. Of gratitude and mercy. Thank you for your place. You've taught me so much. And with that, I bid you farewell. It time to reach people with a new touch. Not of pain and regret, but instead with the warmth of love ill never forget."

# What I Can Control

Emotions change with the weather; just make sure within yourself you hold it together. As the leaves turn brown, make sure to never let down your crown. It is easy to forget who you are when there is the temptation to be swept up by your emotions. Circumstances change as the temperature rises but make sure they don't get the wrong rise out of you. Instead of anger prompting danger, let clarity be a remedy. Something that wasn't there before. Yes, emotions change with the weather, but I know you know best when you hold it together.

Express what needs to be said, nothing more, nothing less. Let them know exactly how you feel and know that with each breath, the message is sent. Take the time to find your footing and your voice. Be ready. Cus' the time will come where you'll have your turn. Your turn to push and pull the tide. Your turn to let out what's inside. It's time now. To allow yourself to feel. Such emotions such range how they change, like the weather. That with the right combination and tone, it can bring others closer together. Or how it can make others afraid. If provoked and placed in the wrong hands, it can bring someone to their knees where they stand. I wouldn't want that for you. To be left stranded with little left to do. Because the ones you trusted with such emotions now fear you. I can assure you.

Your strength brings out another side of you, but it is a responsibility to hold it together. Bringing together logic and reason. Each emotion has its place. Each emotion has its season. And although they change like the weather. I believe in you. To exercise the capacity to hold it together.

# The Art of Projection

Sometimes you're not respected until your voice has been projected. Letting out what's buried deep inside, it seems to me these treasures have long been protected. Having no words to finally being heard is more than any type of liberation. It is clear that we need to put an end to internal suffering. Let it out. Be it by yourself or in front of a crowd. Let it be known. For thoughts and imaginations are meant to be sown.

Everyone is worth this right; it is only right. Arriving at a place where you can finally say what has been bothering you. That you are no longer accepting the mediocre samples life offers you. That you want more for your life. More depth from your relationships because you are worth it. Calling people to their highest selves regardless of what they've been through. That it is possible to come to the end of yourself and let greatness begin.

To shed off the old pain and toxic ways, it never proved to serve you anyway. Sometimes you're taken seriously by others until you take yourself seriously first. It isn't something that begins externally but rather what begins from within. A call to action on how you see yourself. And what does that look like? What does that contain? Because we can no longer own the toxic ways because all they offered was pain. That, in fact, cannot be the fuel to future days. Start by emptying out what has tried to take root.

Come face to face with it one by one and call its name. Deflecting responsibility, communication errors, angry unsolicited outbursts, neglecting your own discomfort, little self-respect and even holding onto past regret. All of these things may be present without us even knowing. That doesn't mean they have permission to keep on growing. Let us dispel them with the tools of patience and honesty. That it may not happen instantly, but it's more than worth it to start getting clean. Clean of the things that no longer serve you or me. Its time to take your well being serious. And once you've gotten used to taking baby steps, it's time to run rapidly. Keep going. Keep growing. Maintain balance and get creative. Be sensitive to yourself and what you need but also how to serve others. An indication of how you love yourself shows up in how you treat your brothers. So be open. Take your message seriously. Don't be afraid to project with all that it comes with. The push back and the resistance are sometimes indications you're on the right track.

# The Standard

There is a higher standard for our lives. That where we are may not be where we will always be. Some may be destined to be Doctors or practice Law. Some may have the dream of animal medicine, and some dreams may not be in this realm at all. Athletics and business may even be a passion that you seek. Others love children and look forward to the opportunity to teach. No matter the passion, no matter the strive, there will always be a challenge to keep that dream alive. Such desires require a resolve.

One that is anchored deep in your soul. One that you'll never let go. That resolve is your reason for doing so. The big "why" that lives in your soul. That when the test comes to shake you up just a little bit. It never puts a dent in your foundation. That this resolve fuels your reason to keep going. To keep growing and keep on showing more and more that you can add to the world with your knowledge. There is a higher standard for our lives.

One that assists our outside world and one that fuels our internal lives. That it also matters the growth that happens on the inside. That our character is also up to the test and that it matters a lot to grow inside. That each battle we face is to make us stronger. That each heartbreak we endure is to make us wiser. That with each loss, it teaches us to make room to give to others. That with each lesson, we change and reach that new standard. That with each goal being met, we will turn to gold. We can do so, even if it takes a lifetime. This is the challenge of life, and this is one we can achieve.

# Face to Face

Why is it so hard to tell you how I really feel? You are so sure of yourself I can hardly tell if this confidence is real. It's remarkable. How anyone human being can do this with such consistency. At such a great pace, precision and potency. I am floored by you. You handle life with such grace, so why is it hard to approach you face to face? I guess you are where I want to be, and I never want to throw you off the ball. I never want to distract you with what goes on with where you are. But it dawned on me, I'll never grow if I always run.

I never want to handle anyone that means a lot to me just for fun. I never want to take their existence for granted. This is the soil in which I plant my tree. To get out of my head and focus on what I need to develop instead. Indeed. The strength I need to get my voice heard and approaching you face to face. With my wants, my needs and my desires, it's about time I articulated such. Not just to you, but to my world and everything in it. Doing so by paying attention to the issues and hand and knocking them down one by one. And it took me a minute to get this confident. I just took an aerial view of what was important to me and how to ultimately get through to you. I had to make an honest assessment.

Measuring each passing moment to make sure if anything went wrong, I'd tell you. I had to separate what went on in my own head and get out of my own way. That no matter how unrealistic it sounded, I couldn't pass up the chance to speak on it. That I admire your grind. Your hustle. Your approach to your world. How I want to be in it. But that takes time. That can only be articulated once we meet face to face.

# Want Vs. Need

It has been known that too much sugar is not good for you. But life without it can be quite bland. That each dose you ever took started with a few pieces in your hand. One piece, two, then maybe three. But if you're not careful, too many pieces and not enough care can result in cavities. Harm came after pleasure because we couldn't take the right measure, on want and not need. It takes time to know the difference. A want is exciting and appeases our senses immediately. It can be anything, really. A want is an inspiration that creeps up with ease.

A pulse that moves rapidly. Causing one's appetite to sway with the wind. Here, no there! Constantly changing. A boat with an anchor and, without the shadow of a doubt, a large sail. A want motivates you to leave the shore and embark on an adventure wanting more. A tall tale of a treasure to be achieved. We know this feeling very well, but what about a need? A Need is quite different. It may not be as exuberating but just as important. For instance, it is important that before a harvest, we must first plant a seed. Such a seed is tedious work, but without it, we cannot benefit from its worth. And it all takes work. For a need first to reveal itself then to be addressed. A need is something that may even require someone else's help.

A need fulfills the soul, and without it getting met, a heart may grow cold. See, the desires of want can swiftly fade away, but if it a need is not meant, the hurt is liable to make a long-lasting stain. A want can fly with the wind, but a need can often sprout from within. Life is to be fulfilled with them both. Needs and wants coincide with one another, allowing life to be worthwhile. But notice not to get them mixed up; it can breed unhealthy desires.

# Let It Be

We've grown apart, and I never knew things would be this way. It's not something I wanted nor something I thought would take easily. My heart has been affected by what has happened, and deep down, I don't want our relationship to be lost in the breeze. I always wondered why we never made amends when we had the chance. Why do we let pride have its way with us denying others a second chance? Away with the way things used to be and start by forgiving. And although this is what I want, I've learned not everyone wants the same thing.

So I had to muster up the courage and let things be. After reaching out and letting it be known how much I care, I won't deny the love was always there. I did my part. I was ready to put it all behind us, but it turned out to be one-sided. The effort was only heavy on one heart. We've grown apart, and I didn't want us to. I'm at a place in my life where I reminisce on where we used to be, and I'll tell the truth. I miss you. I won't deny it. But I've already tried it. Reaching out when it was convenient, attempting to talk face-to-face, and noticing a change in tone in what you said when you really didn't mean it. And I've learned not to dwell on it any longer. No need to make things harder.

Make no mistake, I'm here when you need me. Just fill in the distance things have already be difficult, no need to make them harder. I'll be available and ready to receive your embrace once again. But until then, I've done all that I can. I've decided to give it to God and let it be.

# All You Have

All you have is all you need. Rather than coming from a place of need, learn to look through the lenses of prosperity. That what you have usually started off as a little seed. Even those things can turn into a large tree. One day, one may need what you have and take part in what you are offering. A bright idea, a resource, a helping hand to serve the best that you can. All you have is all you need. Try your best not to compare what is in your hands with what lies in someone else's. That what they've got cant compare to the glory that you hold. That what is unique to you can never grow old. Sometimes these things can start out so small. And sometimes it doesn't make sense at all. One may have five things to start with, all stories untold. Another may have a gift of managing a business from the ground up. These things may be different, but it doesn't mean they are to be compared with their gifting. After all, things are meant to be different. For what each of us is called for, requires different gifting. All you have is all you need. I hope you can identify and battle the limiting beliefs because it's true. All you have is all you need.

# CHAPTER 6
# SHOUT

It is with a shout that messages so deliberate can finally make it out. What a shout does is not only get your message across, but it also has the tendency to shake and alert everyone in its path. Such deliberations can provoke fear or faith in others to share their own stories! But what got us here? What made us shout? The factor of time itself, discomfort in life and the desire to push past limitations with force and conviction.

That such an internal transformation can take place and infect the outside world in a very intentional way. That's what I want for you. To get to a place that you are so tired, get so excited, get so worked up, so amped for what is to come that all there is left to do is shout. I want you to know the liberation and freedom that comes with your breakthrough. That the release on the other side we hear so much about is actually attainable to the common man.

This final section promises to do so as we dive into the topics of fulfilling dreams, the journey to self-love and making amends with the past and coming to terms with things we cannot change. Let this section help you find the freedom that has been there all along. Let it come forth. It's time to let out a ROAR!

# Who do you do it for?

You're too dope. Don't fall back, don't lie down, make 'em see ya'.

Let them be the congregation, and you be the preacher. Oh, Trust me. One day, they'll fall flat on their face, reach out for ya' hand, they g'one need ya'!

How about you be the main event? Spit all the bars and give 'em a feature. Let your truth be nutritious and treat them like babes, be like, "here's a spoon let me feed ya'."

Oh, don't be done yet! And don't be nice! Indulge in virtue and do away with vice. Plant your seeds of wisdom and water your garden by how you do things. But tell me, who do you do it for?

Do you do it for the love of money or the prestige of your brown?
Do you do it for your family? Those back in your hometown?
The young homies? The ghetto? Black grandmas and

black daddies buried 6 feet in the ground?

How about young black bodies etched and outlined in white on the cement? Getting bumped off on this very pavement.

They're dying every day; it's getting too toxic to keep it in because to do so is a sin. So please let me take a minute and vent, tell me, what do you do this for? For the flashing red lights? The Benz? The money? A chance to call the new chick down the way, your new honey? Attention? My brotha' attention? We do all of this for what?!

*For what does it profit a man to gain the whole world but then to lose his soul? Because before you know it, if you're not careful, you'll be labeled a "handful." And in that, you'll want what you were once told. And when you grow old, you'll wanna' go back. But you'll soon look up and find a price tag; your body's been sold.

And your soul's been snatched. But if you look even closer than that, nowadays, all the new slaves aren't just black, and it's sad. I thought we were better than that. I thought we were past all this. Instead, we've added more races to the racist checklist. Doing wrong by my brother and shaming my sister, when will we realize we were never meant to conquer one another? But instead to subdue the earth itself.

That is was our right to be righteous; we were designed this way since birth, our crowns on the top shelf. That there's really enough for everyone, but that's ok…

That's alright, it's cool. I'll keep hope alive until you see. That the evil out there will never have more power than the God living on the inside of me.

# When We In It

Haven't gotten deep in a minute, but once I'm in it, I'm in it. Seeing everyone for everything they got, it's mighty different. How you can change the world with just one touch, in just one instant. That's mighty gifted. Keep praying to God to keep us grounded when we in it. 'Cus when we see the world for the depth we be sinnin'.

It's hard to keep the faith up, keep your distance, 'cus you may drown when you in it. See the hurt, see your world cave in. So be careful. You might be frowning when you in it, but I need you to understand. I need you to see it.

I need you to be fully present, be knee-deep in it. Be committed and lay a crown cross ya' head when you in it. This world that we live in, in this skin we've been given. Each a different tool, each with a different word to save a different fool. Each a different spoon, full of different food. Different reasonings and different seasonings.

Regardless of your difference, remember your

difference is good. It'll be your difference that creates distance making the heavens open up, go crazy. 'Cus you've learned for yourself the truth, the calling on your life could never be fugazi.

Praying to God, whom you've never seen, daily. Throwing up your hands asking Him to work with your "maybes". And trusting whether or not He'd guide you when it gets hazy. But believe me, He runs when He hears the cries of His babies. And I'm in awe each and every time that He'd see me as worth saving. Over and over again, He never ceases to amaze me. I pray the world is no longer ignorant by being so deep that we miss it. The simplicity of your gifting. How we forget the beauty of the innocent. Changing shape and changing the mold, *behold I do a new thing should you not know it?

In Him, He promised we'd never stop growing. The ultimate test is to turn our believing into knowing. Forever hidden to finally showing. Answering the call and completely beholding the truth. The truth that's new to them but was never new to you. That which was always deep down on the inside of you, And I know we haven't gotten deep in a minute, but I invite you to be all in it when you in it. See yourself as mightily different, 'cus you baby are mightily gifted.

# My Chest

You've done it again. You've met me in the place where I hide inside the confines of my insecurities. The chest of treasures buried in my chest has somehow found its way to the fruit of my lips, causing momentum in reality, my excuse?

"I'm only human."

See, I've got a mending problem. You break, I bend only to hold you up with every ounce of my being as I tend to your wounds with every ounce of strength I possess, I'm loyal. But, clearly to a fault, and then you leave because of it. Demons then take their chance to creep inside of my mind and tell me, "it's your fault".

"Too holy, too righteous, too kind, too sweet, you need to slow it down. Switch it up, instead remind them never to play with your heart again." Causing you to swear, urging you to act out of character, out of place, in hopes of making your guardian angels cringe beyond the heavens and outer space. "I'm sorry. But it isn't in my blood".
As I hang my head to wipe every tear rummaging

through the rest of my gems, they have found themselves to be; far too humble, far too graceful, far too quiet.

"Keep this up and you'll always suffer a broken heart. Don't hold onto hope, it'll all be over before it even starts!" They yell louder and louder as they rear their heads in the shape of comparison, "See, you've got to be boisterous like them! Batting large lashes, puckering up your lips, doing away with your waist and swaying your hips!"

This...this could be it. This could be the recipe doing away with all that has plagued me. This could be the mask to cover up my gash, but instead…it isn't in my DNA.

You've done it again. You've exposed me. You've hung onto me like the thorn that nearly killed Paul while he was behind bars accompanied by Silas. *"That which I know to do, but don't do. And that which I do, I shouldn't," it's true.

The flesh IS weak.

The spirit is willing but, why must I endure this constant internal killing? Why? Why was I given this mantle? You know what...take it away, take it back! This calling, this journey, isn't mine to bear. You've got it all wrong, this strength you think I have, I lack...

"Now, hold on", clearly I was interrupted. "my child, I knew you before you knew yourself. I crafted you ,and I knew which ingredients to take off the shelf. This kindness, this loyalty, this meekness, is, in fact, your biggest assets, not at all your weakness. This mantle? Before you knew of it, I gave it to you because I knew it was something you could handle. And just like Paul, that thorn I gave him, I gave to you. Specific in its designs and functions different from anyone else's, proving my grace covers those areas too.

And every time it hurts, my strength is made perfect. Especially when you're down and out and feel as though you're not worth it. Don't hesitate, cry out to me, and I will come running. The chest in your chest I have already emptied and filled with rubies and gems anew. I wonder if then, will they do it again? Trying you and testing you with the same tactics as before. That doesn't matter, draw nigh unto me, and I promise you, it'll be something you're ready for.

This time, as they dig through your chest, they will find the truest treasure; the love that I have for you and the love you have for yourself."

# The Truce

I think it's time I told the truth. It's time I made a truce. Past entities in the form of enemies I made out of distant memories. Things I thought no longer affected me. Strongholds like unforgiveness and regret weighing down on me. For the longest, because of them, I wore a frown. Trying to stay afloat instead of letting myself drown. Self-medicating with bandages wrapping burns and bruises, I thought neglect would solve that last longing problem. But now I think it's time I told the truth. I'm ready to make a truce and go my own way.

Finally having the strength to part and go my own way. Parting ways with senseless arguments and hot-headed dispositions. The plague of paralysis, Depression and regression. Failure and rejection its time we parted ways. Starting today, I did you a favor and let you stay, but now it's time to let go of all the craze. I can no longer make excuses in my head for why I would make such a lofty mistake. But it's ok, I can now tell the truth, I'll be taking all I lost along with this truce. The treasure of time, peace and prosperity are now mine.

Mental and emotional clarity are gems I now know the true value of. That now, if I ever feel the fear of regression, I can look above. I think it's time I told the truth. I didn't arrive at this potency on my own. It took a while. I cried more tears than I had the strength to smile. I had to be reminded of what was always inside me by those called to stand beside me. Looks over my shoulder, ages mine and older and sending me love fighting the urge to grow colder. And I should thank them. They served me what the doctor ordered. Love in a silver spoon.

Hugs. Encouraging words and the enlightenment I was missing. And I would like to take the time, to tell the truth. I wouldn't be where I am had it not been for you. That everything I went through brought me back to a more secure place. That I don't have to go through this alone, this sadness I don't have to face on my own. And I can stand by my crew as I tell the truth. I can now benefit from our truce.

# Faith Over Feelings

Sometimes we are going to be met in life with things that don't always feel right. Things that challenge our comfort or even make us question what's wrong and what's right. These encounters alone are enough to make us go insane. We are liable to throw in the towel and never want to try fighting back again. And although there are times where feeling your feelings is quite necessary, this time isn't one of them. In fact, it's quite contrary. Get out of your feelings.

Feelings can work against what you believe and can work against your seed. For what is meant to grow will soon show in all that you sow. Feelings can explain to the world where you are, but it can stunt your grow if we aren't careful. That the current you're on will always require a necessary flow, and you'll have to fight many of them that don't serve you anymore. Get out of your feelings. Now is not the time to let your depression get in the way of your calling.

You have a gift of healing and helping people win. There's no way you can help someone else but falling into an emotional ditch and giving in. No, you may not see the degree yet, and no, you may not see the breakthrough yet; you already have word that those things are in the works. God's word never returns to Him void, so anything you plant will never be destroyed. Be patient.

Don't let your feelings run you and create an obstructed view. God has a plan, and He's sticking to it. He's wondering if you'll trust him to see you through it. Faith without works is dead. So make sure it's alive instead. By spending enough time in His presence so you can readily dwell on what he said. That when the thunder shakes and the earthquakes. You won't have any reason to be scared. You'll be anchored down, solid, planted and have nothing to fear. So once again, get out of your feeling. Now's the time to make it a habit to choose faith instead.

# Luxury

We deserve to have nice things. You've worked long and hard enough to get the things you truly desire. You should not feel bad for wanting more for your life and your life should finally be reflecting that. That in this life you must be able to go on vacation without feeling bad. Getting a massage without worry about the price tag. We have to fight this mentality that good things are only in the future and cannot be lived for today. That with each passing moment, you get to exercise your say. We deserve nice things along with the love of our life. That a relationship doesn't have to be laced with toxicity or strife.

That you deserve to get it right, even if it's not the first time! That in this time have on earth truth can come to you in your young age. That you can experience the depth of a life long love without being hurt as a prerequisite. Or having to be confused and living in an emotional deficit. No more time can be dedicated to past ways and things that no longer make sense. Past ways never got us here and only held us back. You deserve nice things, and you can finally fight the enemy of lack. No more being bound to a senseless cycle only to survive. In this life, we only have time to thrive with all that God has promised us.

Whatever that looks like, relative to each person, I want that for you. Let's normalize luxury by answering your calling and pushing through what you have to do. Work and then celebrate. Give and continue to create. The world is watching, so I dare you to take this time and be great.

# Self Care

We know it is important to engage in self-care. But what does that really look like, and how do we get there? It seems taboo because all we know how to do well is work until we turn blue. That with each new task, there's a tug on our sanity. Day in and day out, there's a demand on our bodies that weighs us down. Until we finally get this self-care thing down. Each day you have to yourself, take a deep breath. Run bath water and enjoy the hot steam. Light a candle or two and take in the serenity each essential oil has to offer. Close your eyes and take all the time you need. While others love to slow the world down, others like to speed it up by taking a vacation while planning an activity for each day. Trying something new, and eating new foods. Adding to your experiences and expanding your view. And if either scenario isn't how you normally do, you can always take self-care days with a friend or two. Have a night in and enjoy good food. Conversing on what matters and what the world means to you. Self-care comes in so many ways and can be so essential. Make sure to take out time to protect your mental.

# Don't You Worry

Don't worry about who hurt me. Just worry about who no longer has access to me. That, in my silence, I have chosen to value my peace. I have been making a lot of progress. Healing and recognizing what has been bothering me. Neglect and regret, wishing there were things in my past I could change. I was doing a great job, but I hadn't had my breakthrough yet. See, in all my time reframing my mind, I held onto grace just in case you wanted to be a part of my life again. Passivity was normal activity as I wondered in my head why you were watching my movements from the sideline.

Patiently waiting, I thought you'd say something by now. And since you didn't, I can no longer keep making excuses to soften the blow. Your silence is a poor choice of music. We don't have time for any more of this passivity, poor quality of toxic energy. I've gotten ahold of what makes me happy, and although I wish you the best, I know this time is really for the best. You taught me a valuable lesson, and that allows you the space to be your very best. I cannot beg you for what you have yet to learn. So learn what you have to whether or not you choose to return. In the meantime, I will continue to raise my standard and enjoy my peace. It's time I made my boundaries known and fully protected my peace.

# Our Minds

Have healthy conversations. It's time to talk to ourselves by lifting us up instead of tearing each other down. That with each exchange, we are taking the time to fix our crowns. Edifying our spirits and in the wind, you can hear it. A compliment, a kind gesture with no fear to be near it. The power of your mind. I can almost feel it. And this is the difference. Being able to touch those regardless of whose close. There's no competition.

That with each word is spoken to those who are destined to hear it. There's a chance roots will grow and fall on those who are thirsty to know. And I get it, It takes time to do so. Just as we build muscle and gain strength in our physical bodies, it takes reps and consistency. Time's passing and seasons changing. Introducing isolation with each muscle, tendon and tissue. Engaging with each rep tending to a new issue. It's true. Our minds have to the reach same capacity and the same strength as our bodies do. Have healthy conversations. Let's start with how we talk to ourselves. Look at yourself in the mirror and start by the things that you do well. Let yourself know you are proud of where you are and acknowledge now what you want.

What has changed that is something you learned? Do you see love another way? Do you now have a new outlook on life that won't go away? Do you need to forgive someone before going on with your day? Identify what it is. So later on, it isn't in the form of pain that you may have to revisit. Have healthy conversations because our minds are fragile. Even while we aren't awake, we are fighting an ongoing battle. Night after night and day after day, we have to take inventory of what thoughts come in because they turn into the words we say. Out of the abundance of the heart, the mouth speaks. So let's start taking a step back at the things we actively seek. For our minds are fragile, and we are fighting an ongoing battle. Know what you feed it because what comes out does matter.

# Knowledge Vs. Belief

There is a constant battle between what we know and what we believe. That what we've acquired all this time is ready information at your sleeve. Life itself has a course of action that we have yet to achieve. That good things come to those that work hard, grind, and hustle constantly. That this cycle never stops, it never ends! From sun up to sundown, there's a routine that is set up for us to follow. Monday through Friday, eight-thirty to five, dressed in your garb to work at your job. Sitting at your desk, you open up your emails. And soon you'll have a corner desk. Your imagination takes you on a ride; you've made it to the skyline.

The higher you climb, it seems to be time to clock into that meeting. It seems to me you send out cards with seasons greetings. And in the back of your mind, you're thinking, "we've made it". Poverty is not at my back door. Scarcity isn't scary anymore. I need not be afraid of less because there's proof I've achieved more. Meanwhile, each day on your way home, you're still considered the common man with clothes on your back and shoes on your feet. You've provided everything for yourself, yet your disposition proves you are still unhappy. Every need is met with normalcy. Yet you equate it with poverty? And why is that? Why do we do that?

That we should work more to acquire more but until then, we cant be happy. We tend to be focusing more on what we are lacking. And it's true I want more for you. But be content in your right now. You have more now than you did before, and it's a wonderful thing. To be able to dream a new dream. It's for you to hold it, not for it to have a hold on you. Gain new footing on why you want those things. The cars, the clothes, the new fancy bling. Is it because we want to prove to others we are not suffering? That we can afford what we own to hold up to what we said we would achieve? Or is it to give it away to those in need.

More time to speak to those who don't mind listening. Bridging the gap of what you can do by being an example to you and your family. Paving the way to do more in your own community. Do you care about that altruistic feeling? Do you care more about what you give than focusing on what the finances bring? What do you know to do, and what do you believe? Knowing is lives in your head, but your heart is where you truly see.

# It Can Be Overwhelming

Sometimes a dream can be overwhelming. That is the blueprint to breaking generational curses and finally becoming free. And freedom is the one thing we owe to each other and ourselves. For we are not meant to conquer one another but instead the ground itself. Its resources and wealth all enough for one another to benefit; we just need to realize how to manage what was heaven-sent. Laying down one's pride and helping one another with what we don't know. It is this way we know we are sure to grow. And dream. Achieving one's goals no matter how hard it seems. Changing one's taste buds as luxury becomes normalcy.

Let's no longer be afraid of setting the stage for greater. This is king and queen-like behavior. After all, we follow the model of our savior. Isn't it odd that life can get so hard that we are used to one type of behavior? But as we get older, we can grow fonder of new flavors. A new way of life. Finally settling down and realizing you want to get married. Maybe one be a wife. Have children and get a house. It is time to be wise. And dream. Not letting go of what we have already seen. Your pastime is so powerful. It can help set the stage of what can be. Be motivated by the thoughts from within because they prove to be keys to unlock your win. And yes, sometimes a dream can be overwhelming, but what's more earth-shattering is if you never begin.

Start by reasoning with your past. Forgive yourself by making amends with the things that didn't last. Forgive everyone that had their part, and yes, it's hard, but it happened to show the true power of repair after being scarred. Then write it out. Talk with yourself and be open with what you see. How big is the business regardless of the degree? How grand is the nonprofit, how many do you touch in need? Who have you partnered with? For this vision is not simply for "me" but rather achieved with "we". Because yes, a dream can be overwhelming, but with a team and a goal, we can all see it come to pass. We can all reach for the gold.

# Stop Stressing

It is a supreme skill to keep our minds on the present. Mind, body, soul strength, it requires something different to stay where the positivity is. For tomorrow has its own worries and pressures we don't yet need to visit. We'd do ourselves a disservice to bring it into today. That we miss out on the beauty of today. What lies here that we don't think is enough? Our breath, our very existence and reason for living.

How we still have a roof over our heads and an idea in our head. We are far more ahead than we realize. Protect yourself from inviting the pressures of the world that don't need to be there. Be proactive in feeding your mind with positive affirmations. Be specific, and don't shy away from putting yourself as a recipient of greatness.

After all, you need to stop stressing. You need to stay alert and know what's happening in the world. But in doing so, you don't forget the blessing that could change your world. Each moment should start with your favorite thing. What makes you happy? Right here and right now. Be specific and be realistic. When you do that you can get to yourself personally, but you can, but you can articulate it to someone else what it is that fills your cup. T

ake your time. Feel out your environment. Let us know what works and what does not. Let's fix our gaze. For the pressures of tomorrow have no right to ruin our today. This is not to say don't be prepared, but do so just don't get carried away. Reel it back in and let it all melt away. Today is a gift. Enjoy it while you can.

# That Thing

There's something that happens on the inside of us that we can't fake. The desire to get something done that needs our hand in it to make. I've always wanted to be a part of something great. But sometimes, I underestimate what it takes. Long nights and long days, they seem to be the things that weigh me down. Long nights and long days, I wonder if whether or not everyone else is in the same haze. Is it just me? I feel like I'm getting pulled from each direction, yet I wouldn't change it for anything.

There's something that happens on the inside of us that we can't really explain. The inner workings of my mind have caused me to resist the pain. I welcome the hardship and the experience over fame. I want the chance to be a light to those who otherwise could care less about my name. It's something that takes a while to establish but a lifetime to change. And I want it bad. I know I can have it.

After all the ingredients to grab it, live in you too. That thing doesn't have a name, but it has a voice, and I can hear it. If you listen closely, it can speak to your spirit. Finding a deep familiar resolve. It's something that lives in us all.

# Pure Exhortation

I want nothing but the best for you! That what you have to offer; the world needs more of. Your eyes, your mouth, your talent, your heart. All looking for its first time to start. I want you to be able to be free in what God gave you. That there is specifically room for you! That you, too, deserve better. You deserve to embody all that the world has to offer. Yes, challenges happen along the way, but there's a win on the other side with your name. I want to see you smile! I know there's a brighter day in store for you! It's true! That what you've been through isn't the only thing that can keep you. You've got victories in you. Something you've gone through, other people wouldn't know the first thing to do. Be proud of yourself! You got that degree and walked across the stage. You are smart beyond measure; you've accomplished so much regardless of your age. You were able to start that business, and now you're earning six figures. I'm proud of you. If no one has told you, I want to be the first to give an honest review; I'm excited for the rest of all that's in store for you. Just give it time! It's on its way to you.

# Godfidence

You are great, and trust me, they know it too. Sometimes they know it before you do. Some try to stifle your greatness by all the things they put you through. Mental and emotional trauma, even stirring up drama. Trying to make you second guess what's on the inside of you. But enough is enough. Todays the day, they no longer belittle the diamond in the rough. That you can walk into spaces with your head held high and command the room.

All the while speaking highly of your self while starving arrogance. Talking up your brother and your sister and know that they can tap into their Godfidence just like you. No longer is there days that we can excuse someone else's discomfort despite the grace that shines through you. That what makes them uncomfortable has nothing to do with you. Oil and water don't mix and will never share the same point of view.

Don't hold it against them, it's out of our control and something we cant help them do. You are great; trust me, they know it too. And it is for this reason, oftentimes they don't know what to do with you. They are either compelled or repelled by the likeness. Your shine is so bright, many don't know what to do. So many of them try to handle you, and you end up misused. And sometimes, this can cloud your thoughts and obstruct your view. But hear me when I say that even after these moments happen, it still doesn't change your greatness. That the diamond on the inside still holds the potential to shine through. That this Godfidence has never left you. It's just something that you take time to tap into. And when you do, all Hell will try to break loose. Because trust me, you are great, and Hell knows it too.

# Your Story

There's power in your story. That what is to be shared can fall on the ears that care and make a world of difference. That what you've gone through, can, in turn, help the next generation improve. It can be considered. That wisdom is, in a sense is Soul Food. Nutritious in its own way, it can do so much more than just pave the way. That your own story has your truth in it and all that you've experienced. The disappointments you faced and the shortcomings were all orchestrated to reveal God's grace.

That any type of ill fate did not happen and that you were given a second chance. That without a shadow of a doubt, you can give in to what God had planned is quite thought-provoking. How you emerged from a fire destined to harm you yet, you emerged unscathed? How? What went on? What was happening? It is at this moment your story can become your greatest song. Each tune and each turn can either bring up what went right and what went wrong. On and on, it takes time to be able to open up. Replaying each moment and letting them live on. Sometimes looking back hurts, So I'll go first. At a time, I was short on rent. I wasn't getting enough hours at my current job, and the new one I applied for denied me. I was hopeful, in all honesty! I was at this point in my life where I was ready for the new responsibility.

I let down pride and took it upon myself to ask for help. I took notice of my own strength and proceeded to reach up for it myself. Not many do this. But I came to the edge of myself. I took accountability for my situation, yet I still came up short. How could this happen? All I wanted to cry. I felt embarrassed and felt that no one was by my side. I was alone, or so it seemed. And such words I had always known came to me in a dream. "All you have is all you need". And I had faith. The strength to believe. It was small, but it was there. I was indeed very scared, but I've been through worse before. Moving to a new home without a job and being let go one after the other. My self-worth being challenged and wondering when all of this would go under. I was used to taking a huge risk, and I didn't know why. I knew it was in my blood to allow faith to reside.

After all, to this day, it helped me survive. Jump, and the net will appear. So I did. Over and over again. Even when it didn't make sense. But faith often doesn't. In a place of scarcity, we are instructed to give. In a place of depression, turn your mourning into dancing. Turn your silence into a song and praise him all day long. It doesn't make sense, yet it is what we are instructed to do. I've learned this response isn't just for me, but also for those to come after me. The seed deep on the inside of me needs to know the proper response to get free. And yes, some things will happen along the way, but there's power in what happens today. The shortcomings, the worry and the pain. All were meant to ignite someone else's faith. Thank you for listening, and I hope you aren't afraid of the story you hold because it makes you great.

# ABOUT THE AUTHOR

Tamara Faith is a woman of action, but her delivery is what sets her apart from the rest. With a Bachelors of Science in Psychology and a passion for the arts, Tamara has had her hand in understanding the human mind and human emotion ranges. At a young age, she understood that at the core of most interactions, we all just want to be loved and understood.

Tamara has always had a passion for relationships but has always been an advocate for sharing one's individual story, for she believes there's power in each sharing one's voice with the world. Tamara's bubbly and energetic approach to life has always been one of optimism, a poised stature, and uplifting to all that she meets. Her innate ability to instill encouragement to those she meets has made her sought out for a multitude of creative projects and has been sought out as a performer on the stage for her spoken word performances. She has performed at her Alma Mater, Cal State University Northridge, at events such as Espressions, Art 180 and Vocal Artillery. She has also traveled to UCLA speaking on Women Empowerment and back home in Palmdale at a talent show hosted by the Modern Tea House, speaking on Identity and finding one's purpose and encouraging the youth through spoken word at USC LA Prep School.

She has also utilized her talents at Word Play Weekend, Artist Anonymous, Speak Easy Thursdays and most recently First Fridays, and so much more. Tamara has been known to encourage those to follow their dreams and their calling in life as she actively follows hers.

# TAKE THE AWAKEN YOUR VOICE QUIZ!

Tamara Faith wants to help awaken your voice, allowing you to walk in full confidence! When you aren't using your voice, you are showing up small, perhaps coming off as aloof and dismissive to your dreams and feelings. Well, this stops today! Take our quiz so you can do all see what you need to use your voice freely, with courageousness, being secure in who you are.

# VISIT
# TAMARAFAITH.COM
# TODAY!